Charter Sc
in Eight States

Effects on Achievement, Attainment, Integration, and Competition

T0302828

Ron Zimmer, Brian Gill, Kevin Booker, Stephane Lavertu, Tim R. Sass, John Witte

Sponsored by several nonprofit foundations, including the Bill and Melinda Gates Foundation, Joyce Foundation, and William Penn Foundation

RAND EDUCATION

The research in this report was produced within RAND Education, a unit of the RAND Corporation. Funding was provided by several nonprofit foundations, including the Bill and Melinda Gates Foundation, the Joyce Foundation, and the William Penn Foundation.

Library of Congress Cataloging-in-Publication Data is available for this publication.

ISBN 978-0-8330-4693-2

The RAND Corporation is a nonprofit research organization providing objective analysis and effective solutions that address the challenges facing the public and private sectors around the world. RAND's publications do not necessarily reflect the opinions of its research clients and sponsors.

RAND® is a registered trademark.

© Copyright 2009 RAND Corporation

Permission is given to duplicate this document for personal use only, as long as it is unaltered and complete. Copies may not be duplicated for commercial purposes. Unauthorized posting of RAND documents to a non-RAND Web site is prohibited. RAND documents are protected under copyright law. For information on reprint and linking permissions, please visit the RAND permissions page (http://www.rand.org/publications/permissions.html).

Published 2009 by the RAND Corporation
1776 Main Street, P.O. Box 2138, Santa Monica, CA 90407-2138
1200 South Hayes Street, Arlington, VA 22202-5050
4570 Fifth Avenue, Suite 600, Pittsburgh, PA 15213-2665
RAND URL: http://www.rand.org/
To order RAND documents or to obtain additional information, contact
Distribution Services: Telephone: (310) 451-7002;
Fax: (310) 451-6915; Email: order@rand.org

Preface

Charter schools are publicly funded schools that operate outside the direct control of local school districts, under a publicly issued charter that gives them greater autonomy than other public schools have over curriculum, instruction, and operations. The first U.S. charter school opened in 1992, and the scale of the charter movement has since grown to 4,000 schools and more than a million students in 40 states and the District of Columbia. With this growth has also come a contentious debate about the effects of the schools on their own students and on students in nearby traditional public schools (TPSs). In recent years, research has begun to inform this debate, but many of the key outcomes have not been adequately examined, or have been examined in only a few states. We do not know whether the conflicting conclusions of different studies reflect real differences in effects driven by variation in charter laws and policies or, instead, reflect differences in research approaches—some of which may be biased.

This book aims to inform the policy debate by examining four primary research questions in several geographic locations: (1) What are the characteristics of students transferring to charter schools? (2) What effect do charter schools have on test-score gains for students who transfer between TPSs and charter schools? (3) What is the effect of attending a charter high school on the probability of graduating and of entering college? (4) What effect does the introduction of charter schools have on test scores of students in nearby TPSs? We examine similarities and differences in the answers to these questions across locations, seeking insights about the policy levers that might be available to improve the outcomes associated with charter schools.

This research was generously funded by several nonprofit foundations, including the Bill and Melinda Gates Foundation, the Joyce Foundation, and the William Penn Foundation. This is the capstone publication in the study, which previously produced two reports focusing on charter schools in Chicago (Booker, Gill, et al., 2008) and Philadelphia (Zimmer, Blanc, et al., 2008). This monograph builds on the previous work and expands in scope to include additional locations.

This report on the effects of charter schools in different cities and states across the country is consistent with RAND Education's mission—to bring rigorous, objective information to the national debate on education policy. RAND Education identifies new trends, problems, and opportunities and strives to give the policy community and the American public a clearer picture of the choices they face in educating America's citizens.

Contents

Tables

Summary

Charter schools are publicly funded schools that operate outside the direct control of local school districts, under a publicly issued charter that gives them greater autonomy than other public schools have over curriculum, instruction, and operations. Their students (or the students' parents) choose to attend the charter schools rather than being assigned to a school based on residential location. The first U.S. charter school opened in 1992, and the scale of the charter movement has since grown to 4,000 schools and more than a million students in 40 states and the District of Columbia. With this growth has also come a contentious debate. Supporters argue that charter schools can improve student achievement and attainment, serve as laboratories for innovation, provide choice to families that have few options, and promote healthy competition with traditional public schools (TPSs). Critics worry that charter schools perform no better (and, too often, worse) than TPSs, that they may exacerbate stratification by race and ability, and that they harm the students left in TPSs by skimming away financial resources and motivated families.

In recent years, research has begun to inform this debate, but many of the key outcomes have not been adequately examined or have been examined in only a few states. Moreover, questions about the validity of the findings of even the best-designed charter-school impact studies have remained, producing deep uncertainty about the interpretation of results. It has not been clear whether the conflicting conclusions of different studies reflect real differences in effects driven by variation in charter laws and policies or, instead, reflect differences in research approaches—some of which may be methodologically flawed.

We set out to grow the evidence base and inform the debate on charter schools by examining four primary research questions across several geographic locations: (1) What are the characteristics of students transferring to charter schools? (2) What effect do charter schools have on test-score gains for students who transfer between TPSs and charter schools? (3) What is the effect of attending a charter high school on the probability of graduating and of entering college? (4) What effect does the introduction of charter schools have on test scores of students in nearby TPSs? We examine these questions using longitudinal, student-level achievement data from Chicago, San Diego, Philadelphia, Denver, Milwaukee, and the states of Ohio, Texas, and (for question 3 only) Florida. We discuss similarities and differences in charter-school effects across locations, considering whether any observed differences in effects might be related to differences in local charter laws and policies. In conducting these analyses, we also shed light on key research and methodological issues relevant to past and future studies that aim to estimate the achievement effects of charter schools.

What Are the Characteristics of Students Transferring to Charter Schools?

We find no systematic evidence to support the fear that charter schools are skimming off the highest-achieving students. The prior test scores of students transferring into charter schools were near or below local (districtwide or statewide) averages in every geographic location included in the study. In terms of prior achievement, in most sites, the transferring students did not differ substantially from other students in the TPSs they left: In a few sites, they were slightly higher achieving than their former peers; in other sites, they were slightly lower achieving, and, in Ohio and Texas, they were much lower achieving than their former peers. White students, who constituted a minority of charter entrants in all sites, deviated from the general pattern somewhat: In most sites, white students entering charter schools were, on average, slightly higher achieving than the white students in their previous schools.

Transfers to charter schools did not create dramatic shifts in the sorting of students by race or ethnicity in any of the sites included in the study. In most sites, the racial composition of the charter schools entered by transferring students was similar to that of the TPSs from which the students came. There is some variation: Transfers to charter schools tend to marginally reduce racial integration in Philadelphia and in Texas while marginally increasing racial integration in Chicago. We find suggestive evidence that African American students are more likely to self-segregate: African American students transferring to charter schools moved to schools with higher concentrations of African American students in five of seven locales.

What Effect Do Charter Schools Have on Test-Score Gains for Students Who Transfer Between Traditional Public Schools and Charter Schools?

The average effect that charter schools are having on their students across grades K–12 is difficult to estimate, largely because prekindergarten baseline test scores are unavailable to assess the achievement gains of students in elementary charters (as well as K–8 and K–12 charters). For charter schools with entry grades at the middle- and high-school levels (plus a handful of schools that begin in grades 3 and 4), for which we have baseline scores, we have greater confidence in the impact estimates. In five out of seven locales, these nonprimary charter schools are producing achievement gains that are, on average, neither substantially better nor substantially worse than those of local TPSs. In Chicago (in reading) and in Texas (in both reading and math), charter middle schools appear to be falling short of traditional public middle schools. Results that include charter schools at every tested grade level (i.e., those that start in kindergarten as well as those that serve exclusively middle- and high-school grades) are, in most cases, similar to the results that are limited to nonprimary charter schools, providing no evidence that charter-school performance varies systematically by grade level.

The inclusion of kindergarten-entry charter schools in the analysis makes a substantial difference to our estimate of their achievement impacts in only one location. In Ohio, as in most of the other sites, the average performance of nonprimary charter schools is indistinguishable from that of nonprimary TPSs. But when the K-entry charter schools are included in the analysis, the estimated impact of Ohio's charter schools is significantly and substantially negative. The dramatically lower estimated performance of Ohio's K-entry charter schools appears to be attributable not to grade level per se but to virtual charter schools that use technology to deliver education to students in their homes. Virtual schools constitute a large part of the enrollment of K-entry charter schools in Ohio, and students have significantly and substantially lower achievement gains while attending virtual charter schools than they experience in TPSs. This result should be interpreted cautiously, because students who enroll in virtual charter schools may be quite unusual, and their prior achievement trajectories may not be good predictors of their future achievement trajectories.

In most locations, charter schools have difficulty raising student achievement in their first year of operation, typically producing achievement results that fall short of those of local TPSs. This is consistent with prior research and common sense and may not be a charter-specific phenomenon: Opening a new school is challenging, regardless of whether the school is a charter school. Across locations, we see a general pattern of improved performance as schools age.

Finally, charter schools in most locales have marginally greater variation in performance than TPSs, as measured by the achievement-impact estimate for each school, and, in some locations, this may simply reflect greater measurement error associated with the smaller average size of charter schools. Ohio is a notable exception: Its charter schools have a much wider range of variation in performance than its TPSs have.

What Is the Effect of Attending a Charter High School on the Probability of Graduating and of Entering College?

This study was the first to examine the effects of charter schools on long-term attainment outcomes. In the two locations with attainment data (Florida and Chicago), attending a charter high school is associated with statistically significant and substantial increases in the probability of graduating and of enrolling in college. Among students who attended a charter middle school (for whom we can estimate impacts with greater confidence than for charter–high school students who came from conventional public middle schools), those who went on to attend a charter high school were 7 to 15 percentage points more likely to graduate than students who transitioned to a traditional public high school (controlling for observed student characteristics and test scores). Similarly, those attending a charter high school were 8 to 10 percentage points more likely to enroll in college than were their TPS counterparts. In Chicago, the advantage is most clearly evident in the charter high schools that include middle-school grades, eliminating the change of schools between middle and high school. However, readers should keep in mind that we cannot be certain that charter–high school students who attend traditional middle schools also experience these positive effects. Nevertheless, our positive results are promising and are not fully explained by estimated impacts on test scores, suggesting that researchers and policymakers need to look beyond test scores to fully assess charter schools' performance.

What Effect Does the Introduction of Charter Schools Have on Test Scores of Students in Nearby Traditional Public Schools?

There is no evidence in any of the locations that charter schools are negatively affecting the achievement of students in nearby TPSs. But there is also little evidence of a positive competitive impact on nearby TPSs.

What Are the Policy Implications?

A quantitative evaluation of the relationship between charter-school effects and state policy would require data from many more than eight states. Nonetheless, we can inform policy by identifying outcomes that are consistent across sites and by examining outliers in the context of possible policy influences. We emphasize the modifier "possible" in discussing policy influences: Strong causal inferences are difficult in all nonexperimental evaluations, and, with a limited sample of sites and policy variables, policy conclusions must remain tentative.

Findings on the students transferring to charter schools and on the integration effects are largely consistent across sites, suggesting that policymakers need have little fear of cream-skimming or of substantial increases in racial isolation. Relative to local averages, prior achievement levels of charter entrants were particularly low in Texas, which could be attributable (at least in part) to the success of the provision in the state's original charter law encouraging the establishment of charter schools for disadvantaged students.

The overall estimates of the average achievement impacts of charter schools can provide little guidance for policy, given that the validity of the estimates for elementary schools is in doubt. The estimates of the achievement impacts of nonprimary charter schools are more robust to methodological challenges, but they do not show great variation across sites, providing little purchase on the policy levers that might serve to improve the performance of charter schools. Nonetheless, some of the complementary achievement-impact analyses suggest useful guidance:

- Policymakers in every state with a charter law should look for ways to dampen the negative achievement impacts that are so frequently experienced by students enrolled in first-year charters. We cannot provide empirical evidence on specific strategies, but it is easy to imagine possibilities, including working with authorizers to ensure clear plans for the start-up period, providing additional start-up grants to approved operators, or reducing the reliance on brand-new start-up schools by easing the process for existing public or private schools to convert to charter status.

- Policymakers should closely examine the performance of virtual charter schools (in the states where they exist), conducting careful analysis to determine whether their negative achievement trajectories represent underperformance and, if so, identifying ways to improve that performance.
- Policy changes to improve or eliminate the low end of the charter-school performance distribution might be informed by examining the case of Ohio. Among the seven sites in which we conducted achievement analyses, Ohio is the outlier, with an especially wide range of variation. Greater variation in charter performance in Ohio could be related to the fact that the state's charter law allows an unusually diverse group of organizations to serve as charter authorizers (Russo, 2005). It is also possible that the high variation in performance of Ohio's charters is partly related to resource constraints: A Thomas B. Fordham Institute report (2005) found that Ohio's funding scheme for charter schools leaves them at a "severe" disadvantage relative to TPSs.
- Policymakers in Ohio and other states that experience high variation in the performance of charter schools can view this as an opportunity: Eliminating or improving the lowest-performing charter schools has the potential to improve average results substantially. This may not be easy; the challenge is to minimize the number of charter failures without sacrificing successful charter schools. The empirical record does not identify any surefire solutions, but various possibilities could be tried. Improving the performance of charter authorizers, both at the stage of authorization and in subsequent reviews of school performance, would be one place to start.

The promising results of the analysis of long-term effects of charter schools on educational attainment suggest at least two possibilities for policymakers to consider, with potential relevance for TPSs as well as charter schools. First, the favorable results for Chicago's 6–12, 7–12, and K–12 charter schools suggest that school-district leaders and charter-school leaders alike might seriously consider eliminating the school transition between middle school and high school (although the positive results seem to hold up for conventionally configured schools as well). The high-school transition is often a difficult one, and the simple strategy of keeping students in the same schools from seventh grade (or earlier) through 12th grade might reduce the dropout rate—perhaps even if the school is not a charter school. Second, the similarity of the charter attainment results to (some) previous results on Catholic schools suggests the possible value of seeking to replicate characteristics that charter and Catholic high schools have in common. We have no data on the extent to which charter high schools exhibit a similarly coherent mission-driven focus, but the ability to create such schools has often been cited by proponents of charters and other varieties of school choice (see, e.g., P. Hill, Foster, and Gendler, 1990; P. Hill, Pierce, and Guthrie, 1997; Whitman, 2008; and Mathews, 2009). The difference merits consideration by policymakers and further examination by researchers.

The absence of evidence of substantial effects of charter schools on the achievement of students in nearby TPSs might be encouraging to policymakers who were concerned about negative effects and disappointing to policymakers who hoped that competition would induce TPSs to improve. Our findings support the hypothesis (see, e.g., F. Hess, 1999) that charter-school competition is unlikely to create a rising tide of school performance, in the absence of dramatic changes in the structures, incentives, culture, and operation of conventional school districts.

How Should Future Research Evaluate the Performance of Charter Schools?

This study makes clear that there are many bad ways to analyze charter-school performance. The validity of cross-sectional methods that rely on statistical controls for observable student characteristics is cast into doubt by results suggesting that students entering charter schools often have pretransfer achievement levels lower than those of local public-school students who have similar demographic characteristics. Longitudinal methods, such as those used in this study, have many hazards as well, especially when used to assess the performance of charter elementary schools; we therefore rely on them primarily to assess charter middle- and high-school effects.

Finally, one of the most important implications of our work for future research on charter schools is the need to move beyond test scores and broaden the scope of measures and questions examined. Our estimates of positive charter-school effects on high-school graduation and college entry are more encouraging than most of the test score–based studies to date (including our own test-score results). Future studies of charter schools should seek to examine a broad and deep range of student outcome measures and to provide evidence on the mechanisms producing positive long-term impacts.

Acknowledgments

Elaine Allensworth of the Consortium on Chicago School Research and Philip Gleason of Mathematica Policy Research served as technical reviewers for this monograph and provided invaluable comments and suggestions, for which we are grateful. We are also grateful for the effort to develop and provide data from individuals in the various districts and states included in the monograph. In addition, we thank programmers Regan Main and Scott Ashwood along with RAND economist Gema Zamarro for their efforts to clean and manage data sets from various locations. We also appreciate the assistance of RAND senior economist Richard Buddin, who provided helpful suggestions and comments throughout our project, and administrative assistant Robert Hickam for his edits to the document. Finally, we thank the Bill and Melinda Gates Foundation, the Joyce Foundation, and the William Penn Foundation for their generous support in making this study possible.

Abbreviations

EDW	K–20 Education Data Warehouse
FRAG	Florida Resident Access Grant
GED®	General Educational Development Test
ITBS	Iowa Tests of Basic Skills
LEP	limited English proficiency
NAEP	National Assessment of Educational Progress
PSSA	Pennsylvania System of School Assessment
Stanford 9	Stanford Achievement Test Series, Ninth Edition
TAAS	Texas Assessment of Academic Skills
TAKS	Texas Assessment of Knowledge and Skills
TPS	traditional public school
WKCE	Wisconsin Knowledge Concepts Examination

CHAPTER ONE

Introduction

Over the past decade and a half, charter schools have been among the fastest-growing segments of the K–12 education market. Nationally, more than 4,000 charter schools have been established since the early 1990s, and they now serve more than 1 million students. They have spurred a contentious debate since their establishment. Supporters argue that charter schools can improve student achievement and attainment, serve as laboratories for innovation, provide choice to families that have few options, and promote healthy competition with traditional public schools (TPSs). Critics worry that charter schools perform no better than TPSs, that they may exacerbate stratification by race and ability, and that they harm the students left in TPSs by skimming away financial resources and motivated families.

Although research on charter schools is growing, it has only scratched the surface of the important policy questions for the charter movement. For instance, existing studies have generally involved only a single state, and they have not produced consistent findings regarding the relative academic effectiveness of charter schools—which suggests the possibility that charter-school effectiveness may be related to features of the state policy regime in which charter schools operate (Gill, Timpane, et al., 2007).

Moreover, although it is clear that the performance of individual charter schools varies widely, research has not identified the characteristics that distinguish effective charter schools from ineffective charter schools. In addition, the performance of charter high schools has thus far received relatively little attention in existing research. And the research has focused largely on the direct achievement effects of students attending charter schools, with little attention to the systemic effects on students who remain in conventional public schools. Given that charter schools are never likely to enroll more than a minority of the student population in most districts, their systemic effects—positive or negative—may be at least as important as their direct effects. Finally, the existing research has almost exclusively used test scores as measures of performance, ignoring other student outcomes, including measures of educational attainment, such as graduation rates and enrollment in college.

In this monograph, we analyze student-level data from a number of geographic locations across the country to address research questions related to several of these disputes:

- We examine the population of students who are transferring to charter schools to provide evidence on whether charter schools are attracting high- or low-achieving students and to assess the effects of the transfers on racial stratification.
- We assess whether students experience greater achievement gains in charter schools than these same students experience in TPSs and conduct a series of sensitivity tests to inform the ongoing debate about the best ways to assess the achievement impacts of charter schools.
- In Chicago and Florida, we examine longer-term attainment outcomes, analyzing whether charter high schools are increasing (relative to TPSs) their students' likelihood of graduating and their probability of enrolling in college.
- We assess whether there is any evidence that charter-school competition is producing positive or negative effects on the achievement of students who remain in TPSs.

Finally, in the concluding chapter of the monograph, we examine consistencies and differences in the results for each question across different locations, considering the extent to which charter schools are producing similar outcomes in different environments and the extent to which differences in outcomes might be attributable to differences in the details of charter policies.

Geographic Locations Included in the Analysis

We collected data statewide from three states and districtwide from five large, urban school districts. In total, eight states are represented in the data set. Table 1.1 lists each geographic location, the questions addressed (corresponding to the list just presented) and the number of charter schools per site included in the latest year of student achievement data.

Data Description

We collected longitudinally linked student-level data from each location. Table 1.2 lists the years in which charter schools began

Table 1.1
Geographic Locations Included in the Analysis

Geographic Location	Research Question Addressed	Number of Charter Schools Included in the Most Recent Year of Analysis
Chicago: districtwide data	1, 2, 3, 4	33
Denver: districtwide data	1, 2, 4	21
Milwaukee: districtwide data	1, 2, 4	42
Philadelphia: districtwide data	1, 2, 4	57
San Diego: districtwide data	1, 2, 4	35
Florida: statewide data	3	37[a]
Ohio: statewide data	1, 2, 4	246
Texas: statewide data	1, 2, 4	198

[a] In Florida, we included only charter schools that have high-school grades.

Table 1.2
Data Included in the Analysis

Location	School Year in Which Charter Schools Began Operating	Years of K–12 Data	Years of Postsecondary Data
Chicago	1997–98	1997–98 through 2006–07	2002–03 through 2006–07
Denver	1995–96	2001–02 through 2005–06	No data
Milwaukee	1996–97	2000–01 through 2006–07	No data
Philadelphia	1997–98	2000–01 through 2006–07	No data
San Diego	1993–94	1997–98 through 2006–07	No data
Florida	1996–97	1997–98 through 2004–05	2000–01 through 2004–05
Ohio	1998–99	2004–05 through 2007–08	No data
Texas	1996–97	1994–95 through 2003–04	No data

operating and the years of K–12 and postsecondary data we have for each location.

Longitudinal student-level data provide the ability to track students as they move from TPSs to charter schools and vice versa. This allows us to examine not only the effects of charter-school transfers on the mix of students in the different sectors, but also the performance of students before, during, and after attending a charter school. In addition, it permits us to see how the performance of an individual student in a TPS changes as charter schools are introduced nearby.

Included in the data for each student are school identifiers, student grade, race and ethnicity, and test scores in math and reading. High school–graduation and college-entry data were available only in Chicago and Florida. The time frame in which data were collected varied by location. For instance, in San Diego, we were able to collect data from 1997–98 through 2006–07. In contrast, in Ohio, data were available only from 2004–05 through 2007–08.

The most recent year in which we collected test-score data was generally 2006–07. Although we would like to have collected 2007–08 data, this was possible only in Ohio, as the timing of the publication was not conducive to collecting and analyzing more-recent data across all locations.

We provide a more-detailed description of each of the data sets in Appendix A, which includes information about any exclusions we made in the data sets and how we classified schools. In addition, in our description of our analysis in later chapters, we describe some of the challenges and nuances of the data sets.

CHAPTER TWO

Students Transferring to Charter Schools

We begin with a descriptive examination of students transferring to charter schools. Critics of charter schools fear that they will further racially or ethnically[1] stratify an already deeply stratified system and will skim off the best students from TPSs, harming the students left behind. In contrast, some charter supporters hope that charter schools will improve racial integration by letting families choose schools outside of neighborhoods where housing is racially segregated. Integration may be an important policy outcome in its own right, and evidence suggests that the interaction with diverse backgrounds and ability levels can have positive social and academic effects for students (Frankenberg and Lee, 2003; Zimmer and Toma, 2000; Summers and Wolfe, 1977).

Several studies have examined the racial representativeness of charter schools (Powell et al., 1997; Miron and Nelson, 2002; Frankenberg and Lee, 2003). These studies have generally needed to rely on school-level data rather than student-level data and have examined whether the racial composition of charter schools is similar to that of the districts or states where they are located. They have not examined the actual counterfactual for the charter students—what would have been the racial composition of the school the students would have attended if they had not transferred to a charter school? Nor did these studies examine whether the charter schools are skimming off the cream—the highest-achieving students from the TPSs.

[1] For simplicity, we use the term *race* instead of *race/ethnicity*.

To address these questions, researchers need longitudinally linked student-level data, which provides the ability to follow students as they transfer from TPSs to charter schools. Previously, Bifulco and Ladd (2007) examined migration patterns of students choosing to transfer to a charter school. They found that African American students in North Carolina were likely to switch to charter schools with higher concentrations of African American students than the TPSs that they left. This charter-school migration increased the racial isolation of African American students. We build on the models used by Bifulco and Ladd to examine the distributional effects of charter schools across the locations.

Prior Achievement of Students Transferring to Charter Schools

First, we examine the prior achievement levels of students who enter charters, as compared with average districtwide achievement levels and with the achievement levels of other students in the TPSs from which they transferred. This analysis examines only students who switch into charter schools after they have been in TPSs. Because test scores are not available for students prior to kindergarten, it is impossible for us to test whether charter elementary schools are attracting the best students at the entry point. In addition, the analysis removes students who are making structural moves—i.e., students who are switching from elementary to middle school and middle to high school—because, for such students, their previous school is no longer the relevant counterfactual (and we do not have data to indicate the TPS they would have attended if they had not attended the charter school). But we also conducted alternative analyses that included structural movers (on the assumption that the average achievement levels in their previous schools might be unbiased, if noisy, proxies for average achievement levels in the unknown counterfactual schools), and the results were quite consistent with those shown in Table 2.1, with no substantive differences in any of the sites.

Table 2.1
Average Prior Math and Reading Scores of Charter Movers and Other Students at the Traditional Public Schools That They Leave

Variable	Overall	White Students	African American Students	Hispanic Students
Chicago				
Prior math scores of movers	−0.03	0.30	−0.05	0.06
Prior math scores of TPS peers	−0.12	0.36	−0.17	0.03
Difference with TPS peers	0.09	−0.06	0.12	0.03
Prior reading scores of movers	0.02	0.35	0.01	0.02
Prior reading scores of TPS peers	−0.09	0.36	−0.12	−0.03
Difference with TPS peers	0.11	−0.01	0.13	0.05
Denver				
Prior math scores of movers	−0.32	0.16	−0.45	−0.34
Prior math scores of TPS peers	−0.16	0.13	−0.13	−0.25
Difference with TPS peers	−0.16	0.03	−0.32	−0.09
Prior reading scores of movers	−0.25	0.47	−0.18	−0.33
Prior reading scores of TPS peers	−0.17	0.22	−0.04	−0.29
Difference with TPS peers	−0.08	0.25	−0.14	−0.04
Milwaukee				
Prior math scores of movers	−0.02	0.61	−0.33	0.10
Prior math scores of TPS peers	−0.01	0.28	−0.15	0.05
Difference with TPS peers	−0.01	0.33	−0.18	0.05
Prior reading scores of movers	−0.04	0.52	−0.29	0.02
Prior reading scores of TPS peers	−0.04	0.21	−0.16	−0.02
Difference with TPS peers	0.00	0.31	−0.13	0.04

Table 2.1—Continued

Variable	Overall	White Students	African American Students	Hispanic Students
Philadelphia				
Prior math scores of movers	−0.11	0.47	−0.16	−0.20
Prior math scores of TPS peers	−0.17	0.26	−0.21	−0.20
Difference with TPS peers	0.06	0.21	0.05	0.00
Prior reading scores of movers	−0.05	0.53	−0.08	−0.23
Prior reading scores of TPS peers	−0.18	0.22	−0.19	−0.25
Difference with TPS peers	0.13	0.31	0.11	0.02
San Diego				
Prior math scores of movers	−0.29	0.11	−0.54	−0.43
Prior math scores of TPS peers	−0.12	0.10	−0.22	−0.21
Difference with TPS peers	−0.17	0.01	−0.32	−0.22
Prior reading scores of movers	−0.20	0.28	−0.42	−0.41
Prior reading scores of TPS peers	−0.11	0.14	−0.21	−0.23
Difference with TPS peers	−0.09	0.14	−0.21	−0.18
Ohio[a]				
Prior math scores of movers	−0.61	−0.33	−0.89	−0.60
Prior math scores of TPS peers	−0.41	−0.13	−0.68	−0.51
Difference with TPS peers	−0.20	−0.20	−0.21	−0.09
Prior reading scores of movers	−0.56	−0.30	−0.80	−0.51
Prior reading scores of TPS peers	−0.41	−0.14	−0.65	−0.49
Difference with TPS peers	−0.15	−0.16	−0.15	−0.02

Table 2.1—Continued

Variable	Overall	White Students	African American Students	Hispanic Students
Texas				
Prior math scores of movers	−0.46	−0.03	−0.83	−0.47
Prior math scores of TPS peers	−0.24	0.02	−0.41	−0.27
Difference with TPS peers	−0.22	−0.05	−0.42	−0.20
Prior reading scores of movers	−0.38	0.11	−0.64	−0.47
Prior reading scores of TPS peers	−0.21	0.07	−0.32	−0.31
Difference with TPS peers	−0.17	0.04	−0.32	−0.16

[a] Because Ohio has virtual schools, which are fairly unusual, we also ran the analysis excluding virtual schools. The results for all students, for African American students, and for Hispanic students are very similar. For white students, the patterns are similar but with slightly smaller differences.

Table 2.1 shows the average standardized prior math and reading scores of charter movers and of their peers within the same grade at the TPSs the movers exited for each district. Original scores are scaled scores from state accountability tests or district-administered tests. To make the results comparable across grades and subjects and across geographic locations, we standardized them relative to the districtwide or statewide distribution in each grade and subject. Therefore, scores in the table are standardized z-scores, with negative scores below the districtwide or statewide average and positive scores above.

In some locations, the differences in test scores between those who move to charter schools and their peers who remain in TPSs are small. For instance, in Chicago, Philadelphia, and Milwaukee, students who switched to charter schools had prior test scores that were generally slightly lower than district averages (as evidenced by the negative z-scores) but either identical to or slightly higher than the scores of their peers in the TPSs they exited. In Denver and San Diego, students transferring to charter schools had prior test scores that were not only below districtwide averages but also lower than those of the students in the TPSs they exited.

In Ohio and Texas, these differences are more pronounced. In each of these locations, students transferring to charter schools have test scores that are substantially below state averages and the average scores of the peers in the TPSs they exited. Note, however, that the standardized scores in Ohio and Texas should not be compared directly with those in the other sites. Charter schools often tend to locate in low-achieving school districts, so statewide average scores may be substantially higher than districtwide scores (thereby producing lower relative z-scores).

In sum, in all but one case (Chicago reading scores, which are virtually identical to the districtwide average), students switching to charter schools had prior test scores that were below districtwide or statewide averages (though usually the difference was small). Compared with their immediate peers in the TPSs they exited, students transferring to charter schools had slightly higher test scores in two of seven locations, while, in the other five locations, the scores of the transferring students were identical to or lower than those of their TPS peers. Same-race comparisons indicate lower prior scores for charter students in five of seven sites among African Americans and in four of seven sites among Hispanics. For white students, the pattern was slightly different: In four of seven sites, white students entering charter schools had higher prior achievement than their white peers, and, in one other site, they had higher scores in one of two subjects. These results for white students had little effect on the overall averages because white students constituted a minority of charter students in every location and less than one-quarter of charter students in the four locations where their scores were consistently higher than those of their white peers (as we show in the next section).

Transfers to Charters and Racial and Ethnic Stratification

In this section, we compare the racial composition of the sending (traditional public) and receiving (charter) schools of students transferring to charters. Before presenting the results, we provide context with a descriptive breakdown of three major groups of students in charter and

TPSs in Table 2.2. African American students are overrepresented in charter schools in six of seven locations, which is consistent with previous research (Bifulco and Ladd, 2007; Booker, Zimmer, and Buddin, 2005). Patterns for white students and Hispanic students are more mixed, varying across sites.

The data in Table 2.2 are useful for understanding aggregate representation of different racial groups across the charter and TPS sectors in the different locations, but they do not tell us about the relative levels of integration in charter schools and TPSs, because sectorwide numbers could mask enormous variation in the integration of individual schools. The 40-percent share of San Diego's charter enrollment represented by Hispanic students, for example, could result from Hispanics constituting 40 percent of the enrollment of every charter school in San Diego, or it could result from Hispanics constituting 100 percent of the enrollment of 40 percent of the charter schools and zero in the rest. Moreover, the data in Table 2.2 do not tell us about the effects on integration of students transferring into charter schools

Table 2.2
Charter and Traditional Public School Racial Representation Across All Years in Our Data (%)

	Charter School			TPS		
Location	African American	White	Hispanic	African American	White	Hispanic
Chicago	72.9	2.7	23.5	52.7	9.4	34.8
Denver	31.7	20.4	44.8	19.6	20.0	56.0
Milwaukee	40.7	23.0	27.1	63.8	14.1	14.4
Philadelphia	66.1	19.3	12.3	64.2	15.2	14.8
San Diego	22.9	20.4	40.4	14.5	27.1	39.4
Ohio	55.3	38.7	2.6	15.4	77.9	2.5
Texas	35.8	22.5	39.4	15.7	42.4	39.2

NOTE: Percentages do not all sum to 100 because some students do not fit these categories.

because they do not tell us where the students would have been if they had not transferred.

Table 2.3 attempts to shed light on these issues by comparing the peer environments (in racial terms) for charter movers before and after moving to a charter school, separately for African American students, Hispanic students, and white students. (Totals across rows may not add up to 100 percent because other racial categories are omitted, but those categories constituted only small minorities in most sites.)

Table 2.3
Traditional Public and Charter Peer Environments for Charter Movers, by Racial and Ethnic Background of Student (%)

Variable	African American	White	Hispanic
Chicago			
Charter school that African American students attend	84.3	2.1	13.2
TPS that African American students attended	89.9	2.3	7.0
Difference	–5.6[a]	–0.2	6.2
Charter school that white students attend	55.7	11.8	29.8
TPS that white students attended	26.3	20.1	40.6
Difference	29.4	–8.3[a]	–10.8
Charter school that Hispanic students attend	44.0	5.3	49.3
TPS that Hispanic students attended	18.2	8.6	70.1
Difference	25.8	–3.3	–20.8[a]
Denver			
Charter school that African American students attend	51.0	14.6	31.0
TPS that African American students attended	42.2	15.3	41.9
Difference	8.8[a]	–0.7	–10.9

Table 2.3—Continued

Variable	African American	White	Hispanic
Charter school that white students attend	32.1	31.0	31.6
TPS that white students attended	25.2	28.7	38.9
Difference	6.9	2.3[a]	–7.3
Charter school that Hispanic students attend	21.9	11.6	64.0
TPS that Hispanic students attended	15.7	9.0	72.1
Difference	6.2	2.6	–8.1[a]
Milwaukee			
Charter school that African American students attend	65.5	13.2	13.8
TPS that African American students attended	73.0	10.5	9.7
Difference	–7.5[a]	2.7	4.1
Charter school that white students attend	27.4	38.9	23.0
TPS that white students attended	29.2	38.3	21.5
Difference	–1.8	0.6[a]	1.5
Charter school that Hispanic students attend	26.2	23.9	40.0
TPS that Hispanic students attended	25.5	19.2	47.0
Difference	0.7	4.7	–7.0[a]
Philadelphia			
Charter school that African American students attend	87.0	4.6	6.9
TPS that African American students attended	84.2	5.5	7.0
Difference	2.8[a]	–0.9	–0.1
Charter school that white students attend	36.1	48.7	10.9

Table 2.3—Continued

Variable	African American	White	Hispanic
TPS that white students attended	39.5	39.7	12.3
Difference	–3.4	9.0[a]	–1.4
Charter school that Hispanic students attend	35.5	6.9	55.9
TPS that Hispanic students attended	38.1	12.0	45.4
Difference	–2.6	–5.1	10.5[a]
San Diego			
Charter school that African American students attend	33.7	20.0	32.1
TPS that African American students attended	25.3	16.1	39.2
Difference	8.4[a]	3.9	–7.1
Charter school that white students attend	15.8	42.1	30.2
TPS that white students attended	12.5	39.0	32.3
Difference	3.3	3.1[a]	–2.1
Charter school that Hispanic students attend	17.2	22.2	50.5
TPS that Hispanic students attended	15.8	19.0	49.4
Difference	1.4	3.2	1.1
Ohio[b]			
Charter school that African American students attend	78.9	16.5	2.1
TPS that African American students attended	74.1	20.0	3.0
Difference	4.8[a]	–3.5	–0.9
Charter school that white students attend	17.0	77.0	2.4
TPS that white students attended	14.9	79.0	3.1

Table 2.3—Continued

Variable	African American	White	Hispanic
Difference	2.1	–2.0[a]	–0.7
Charter school that Hispanic students attend	38.5	40.9	14.8
TPS that Hispanic students attended	31.8	42.1	21.6
Difference	6.7	–1.2	–6.8[a]
Texas			
Charter school that African American students attend	67.1	12.3	19.8
TPS that African American students attended	52.4	14.4	31.7
Difference	14.7[a]	–2.1	–11.9
Charter school that white students attend	17.3	54.8	24.2
TPS that white students attended	15.6	50.4	30.3
Difference	1.7	4.4[a]	–6.1
Charter school that Hispanic students attend	19.7	13.7	63.2
TPS that Hispanic students attended	15.1	12.4	71.4
Difference	4.6	1.3	–8.2[a]

[a] The percentage difference between the school a student exits and the school the student enters in the student's own race or ethnicity.

[b] Because Ohio has virtual schools, which are fairly unusual, we also ran the analysis excluding virtual schools. The results show similar patterns but are slightly more pronounced.

As is the case with Table 2.1, this analysis examines only students who switch into charter schools after they have been in TPSs. We do not have data that would allow an examination of what the racial composition would have been in a TPS for students who never attended TPSs—most importantly, students who begin in charter schools in kindergarten. Also, the analysis removes students who are making structural moves because the prior TPSs may not represent a strong counterfactual for the racial makeup of the school that the students would have attended in the later grade level had they not chosen a charter.

In most cases, the results in Table 2.3 suggest that (on average) transferring students are moving to charter schools with racial compositions that do not differ dramatically from those of the TPSs they left behind. Across the sites, however, African American transfer students are slightly more likely than white students or Hispanic students to move to charter schools that have larger proportions of their own racial group. This does not necessarily indicate a preference for a same-race environment; it could result simply from a preference among African Americans for charter schools (in which they tend to be overrepresented, as shown in Table 2.2). In five of the seven sites, African American students transferred to charter schools with (on average) higher concentrations of African Americans than were present in the TPSs they exited. Across the seven jurisdictions, the (unweighted) average increase in the African American concentration experienced by an African American transfer student was 3.8 percent, versus an average increase of 1.3 percent in the white concentration experienced by transferring white students and an average decline of 5.9 percent in the Hispanic concentration experienced by transferring Hispanic students.

Some differences are also evident across jurisdictions. Philadelphia is the only site where transferring students of all three groups tend to move to charter schools with higher concentrations of their own race. In Chicago, in contrast, transferring students of all three groups tend to move to charter schools with *lower* concentrations of their own race. In all of the other sites, the results vary for different racial groups. Across 21 comparisons (seven sites with three racial groups each), we find only two cases in which the average difference between the sending TPS and the receiving charter school is greater than 10 percentage points in the concentration of the transferring student's race.

Chapter Summary

Overall, across the two analyses, it does not appear that charter schools are systematically skimming high-achieving students or dramatically affecting the racial mix of schools for transferring students. Students transferring to charter schools had prior achievement levels that were generally similar to or lower than those of their TPS peers. And transfers had surprisingly little effect on racial distributions across the sites: Typically, students transferring to charter schools moved to schools with racial distributions similar to those of the TPSs from which they came. There is some evidence, however, that African American students transferring to charters are more likely to end up in schools with higher percentages of students of their own race, a finding that is consistent with prior results in North Carolina (Bifulco and Ladd, 2007).

CHAPTER THREE

Student Achievement in Charter Schools

In recent years, studies have attempted to examine the impact of charter schools on student achievement in Arizona (Solmon, Paark, and Garcia, 2001), California (Zimmer, Buddin, et al., 2003; Betts, Rice, et al., 2006; Zimmer and Buddin, 2006), Florida (Sass, 2006), Massachusetts (Abdulkadiroglu et al., 2009), Michigan (Bettinger, 2005), Ohio (Ohio Department of Education, 2007), New York (Hoxby and Murarka, 2007), North Carolina (Bifulco and Ladd, 2006), Texas (Hanushek et al., 2005; Booker, Gilpatric, et al., 2007), Wisconsin (Witte et al., 2007), and Pennsylvania (Zimmer, Blanc, et al., 2008). In addition, a few recent studies have examined student achievement in charter schools nationally (Nelson, Rosenberg, and Van Meter, 2004; Hoxby, 2004).

Distinguishing the effects of schools from the effects of family and other external factors is challenging under any circumstances, and it is especially problematic in evaluating charter schools, where students are likely to differ from those in TPSs simply because they have chosen to attend charter schools. Differences between choosing and nonchoosing students may be related to achievement in positive or negative ways, thereby producing selection bias in comparing achievement in charter schools and TPSs.

Researchers have dealt with the selection bias in charter enrollment in three ways: randomized experiments, longitudinal analyses, and cross-sectional comparisons that attempt to match school and student characteristics or control statistically for their differences. The first two methods allow researchers to account for the amount of time a student has spent in a particular school, and all three methods attempt to address differences among student populations served.

Randomized experiments are often considered the gold standard in research because, by assigning subjects randomly to the treatment condition or control condition, they ensure that differences observed later are the result of treatment rather than the result of background differences between the subject groups. A few studies are beginning to examine oversubscribed charter schools that randomly admit students through lotteries. For instance, Hoxby and Rockoff (2004) found that four Chicago charter schools that admitted students by lottery were outperforming TPSs as measured by students' subsequent achievement. Later, Hoxby and Murarka (2007) used a similar design to evaluate 47 charter schools in New York City and likewise found a small positive achievement effect for students attending charter schools. Abdulkadiroglu et al. (2009) found that a subset of charter middle and high schools in Boston that used admission lotteries also found positive impacts (sometimes large). And Mathematica Policy Research is engaged in a federally funded national study of oversubscribed charter middle schools that admit students by lottery; results are not yet available (see Mathematica Policy Research, undated).

These lottery-based studies have strong *internal* validity: Researchers can be confident that the participating charter schools caused the achievement advantages for the students who were admitted in their lotteries. But although the studies should produce internally valid and reliable results for the set of charter schools and students examined, they may have limited implications for charter schools that lack lengthy waiting lists and do not use lotteries to admit students. In other words, these studies have weak *external* validity. Charter schools with lengthy waiting lists might well be those that are better than average. Indeed, the only study that has begun to examine the issue found that charter schools using admission lotteries appeared to be more effective than charter schools that were not oversubscribed (Abdulkadiroglu et al., 2009).

When researchers have attempted to be more inclusive in their analysis of charter schools, some have relied on school-level data or cross-sectional student-level comparisons of achievement in charter schools and TPSs at a single point in time (e.g., Nelson, Rosenberg, and Van Meter, 2004; Hoxby, 2004). A key weakness of a school-level analysis is the high degree of aggregation, which masks changes over time in the school's population. In essence, school-level data may not pick up the nuances of student characteristics and can provide only an incomplete picture of why outcomes vary across schools. Moreover, school-level data are especially problematic when used to compare changes over time in the performance of charter schools versus TPSs. As we discuss later, there is good evidence that charter schools often have a negative achievement effect in their first year of operation. The spring of a charter school's first year of operation, which is the earliest possible starting point for a longitudinal analysis of schoolwide data, is, therefore, an artificially low baseline.

Meanwhile, point-in-time data, even at the student level, cannot account for the amount of time spent in different schools and may not be able to factor out the various nonschool factors that affect student achievement. Students who choose to attend charter schools are likely to differ from TPS students in unobservable ways that are not fully captured in demographic characteristics, such as poverty and race. They might have better-informed and more-motivated parents than TPS students of the same poverty level and race. Or they might be students who have had difficulties in school in the past and seek out charter schools because they have not done well in TPSs. If either of these stories is true, then adjusting for observed characteristics, such as race and poverty, in a cross-sectional analysis would produce an estimate of charter-school impacts that is biased upward or downward.

As an alternative nonexperimental approach, researchers have often used longitudinal data at the student level to conduct within-student comparisons of achievement gains, examining changes in the achievement trajectories of individual students who move from TPSs to charter schools or vice versa. This method allows the researcher to account for unobservable differences as well as observable differences between charter students and noncharter students, as long as those differences are *fixed*, i.e., consistent across time in their effects on achievement. This approach was endorsed by a collection of research experts known as the Charter School Achievement Consensus Panel (Betts and

Hill, 2006). To date, a handful of studies have used a within-student longitudinal approach to evaluate charter schools in individual states and cities: Solmon, Paark, and Garcia (2001) in Arizona; Bifulco and Ladd (2006) in North Carolina; Gronberg and Jansen (2001) in Texas; Hanushek et al. (2005) in Texas; Booker, Gilpatric, et al. (2007) in Texas; Zimmer, Buddin, et al. (2003), Betts et al. (2006), and Zimmer and Buddin (2006) in California; Sass (2006) in Florida; Witte et al. (2007) in Milwaukee. These studies have produced mixed results in terms of estimates of the achievement effects of charter schools.

Because we do not have charter-school wait lists to conduct a randomized design, we build on this existing literature and use a longitudinal, within-student analysis known as a *student fixed-effect approach*. The student fixed-effect approach has recently been subject to questions about its validity in producing unbiased estimates of charter-school impacts (Hoxby and Murarka, 2006; Ballou, Teasley, and Zeidner, 2007), and we conduct several specification tests and make changes to our analyses to address these concerns. Three concerns about the validity of the student fixed-effect approach are notable.

First, the student fixed-effect approach depends on the assumption that students' past gain trajectories are good predictors of future gain trajectories. Hoxby and Murarka (2006) argue that students who transfer to charter schools in the middle of their educational careers may be those who had unusual difficulties in the immediately preceding year—difficulties that reflect a time-specific change in their likely future achievement trajectories. If so, the fixed-effect approach could produce biased estimates. Moreover, if a bias exists, its direction is not obvious a priori. If the pretransfer dip represents a transitory change—i.e., the student had one anomalously difficult year—then we would expect the dip to be temporary, and the estimate of the charter school's impact would be inflated as the student's scores regressed toward their long-term mean. If, by contrast, the pretransfer dip represents a change in the student's long-term trajectory, then long-term prior achievement might overestimate the student's future achievement, and the estimate of the charter school's effects would be correspondingly biased low.

The second and related concern is that the fixed-effect approach provides an estimate of student achievement only for students who switch from a TPS to a charter school or vice versa (*switchers*). Students who remain in charter schools for the duration of the analysis do not contribute to the estimate because their achievement gains in charter schools cannot be compared to their achievement gains in TPSs. Switchers may differ from nonswitchers (or *stayers*) in important ways. If so, this could undermine the external validity of the results: Results that are accurate for the switching students might not predict results for stayers.[1]

Third, the student fixed-effect method assumes that any deviation in a student's achievement trajectory is attributable to the school the student is currently attending and that charter-school effects can be estimated based not only on the students who transfer into charter schools but also on those who transfer out. This assumption helps to address the previous concern: More students who switch schools at natural entry and exit grades can be included in the analysis. But it is a strong assumption that is particularly important for estimating the impacts of charter elementary schools, where students entering in kindergarten do not contribute to the impact estimate but students exiting to traditional middle (or high) schools do contribute. In essence, the student fixed-effect method estimates the effect of a student's previous charter school by differencing out the student's subsequent TPS results in the same way that it estimates the effect of a student's current charter school by differencing out the student's previous TPS results. In other words, the analysis assumes chronological reversibility. If the reversibility assumption is invalid, the student fixed-effect method could produce biased results, especially for elementary schools, where impact estimates must derive disproportionately from students who graduate to traditional middle and high schools.

---

[1] Ballou, Teasley, and Zeidner (2007) explore these issues by examining Idaho charter schools both by using a student fixed-effect model, which uses only switchers, and by estimating the effect using all tested charter and noncharter students. Exploring both approaches, they find conflicting results. The authors argue that the bias from examining only switching students in a student fixed-effect model may be greater than the self-selection bias the model attempts to correct and may imply that researchers should not rely exclusively on fixed-effect models.

To the extent possible, we examine these concerns empirically. We conduct sensitivity analyses that examine whether students who switch into charter schools experience a dip in achievement prior to entering a charter school and whether switchers have differential annual gains from those of students who are observed only in charter schools. We also conduct an alternative analysis focusing exclusively on charter middle and high schools—i.e., schools in which all students are switchers.

Analytical Details

As previously discussed, outcome indicators for the achievement analyses are math and reading z-scores for individual students followed longitudinally over time.[2] The longitudinal nature of the data allows the use of a student fixed effect to control for any time-invariant characteristics of the student, such as family status and ability. The fixed-effect model is implicitly a value-added model that aims to assess the contribution of attending a charter school.

The formal model for our analysis is specified in Equation 3.1.[3] To examine achievement effects, we use achievement gains $\left(A_{jt} - A_{jt-1}\right)$ for individual students as the outcome of interest. Using gains allows the analysis to compare the student's achievement gains while attending a charter school with his or her achievement gains while not attending a charter school. Examining gains accounts for the possibility that students with similar baseline achievement scores have different underlying achievement trajectories. Formally, the model is specified as

---

2 As indicated in Chapter Two, these z-scores are scaled scores from state accountability tests or district-administered tests. To make the results comparable across grades and subjects and across geographic locations, we standardized them relative to the districtwide or statewide distribution in each grade and subject.

3 The analysis incorporates the clustering of student achievement results within schools, thereby ensuring the estimation of robust standard errors.

$$A_{jt} - A_{jt-1} = \alpha C_{jt} + \pi Mob_{jt} + \mu_j + \theta_{gt} + \nu_{jt}, \qquad (3.1)$$

where $A_{jt} - A_{jt-1}$ is a measure of the achievement gain of the *j*th student in the *t*th year; C_{jt} is an indicator of whether student *j* attend a charter school in the *t*th year; Mob_{jt} is an indicator of whether student *j* transferred to a new school in the *t*th year; μ_j captures individual student fixed effects; θ_{gt} captures grade-by-year fixed effects; and ν is the random disturbance term.

We followed the lead of Hanushek et al. (2005) by including a mobility dummy variable. We include the mobility variable so that our achievement analysis can be representative of charter students who are not part of our analysis because they have never switched between a charter school and TPS. Without this control, we are less likely to represent their experience.[4] By including the control, we implicitly assume that switching schools is not a necessary part of the charter treatment—i.e., that many students can enter charter schools at grade levels that would have involved a change of schools even if the students had remained in TPSs (e.g., moving from elementary to middle or middle to high school). For students who enter charter schools at grades when they could have otherwise avoided switching schools (had they stayed in their prior TPS), the net impact of the shift would include any negative shock associated with the school shift itself; such students would benefit from switching schools only if the cumulative effect of attending the charter school ultimately exceeded any negative effect associated with mobility. Our impact estimates are intended to capture the charter effect net of mobility.

Although Equation 3.1 provides an overall estimate of charter-school effects, we are also interested in the effects over time and by types of students. Therefore, we modified Equation 3.1 to carry out additional analyses.

---

[4] The coefficient estimate for the mobility variable is driven primarily by students who switch from TPS to TPS and not by students who switch between a TPS and charter school or from charter school to another charter school. The vast majority of students switching schools are switching between TPSs.

First, a variation of Equation 3.1 is used to examine the effects by the year of operation of charter schools. Specifically, we examine the effect for students attending a charter school in operation for one, two, or three or more years. Previous research suggests that student achievement may improve as charter schools mature (Booker, Gilpatric, et al., 2007; Bifulco and Ladd, 2006; Sass, 2006). The formal model for the analysis is specified in Equation 3.2, in which *YRone* takes on the value of 1 when the student attends a charter school in the first year of operation and 0 otherwise; *YRtwo* takes on the value of 1 when the student attends a charter school in the second year of operation and 0 otherwise; and *Mult* takes on the value of 1 when the student attends a charter school in the third or more year of operation and 0 otherwise.

$$A_{jt} - A_{jt-1} = \alpha YRone_{jt} + \phi YRtwo_{jt} + BMult_{jt} + \pi Mob_{jt} + \mu_j + \theta_{gt} + \nu_{jt}. \quad (3.2)$$

Second, Equation 3.1 is expanded to include an interaction term (*R*) to examine whether the achievement effects of charters vary across racial or ethnic categories. More specially, we created four dummy variables of the interaction between indicators of attending a charter school in a particular year and being African American, white, Hispanic, or of some other race or ethnicity. While a student's race or ethnicity does not change over time, his or her charter status can, which identifies the effect of charter-school attendance for students of each race or ethnicity. The expanded model is displayed in Equation 3.3:

$$A_{jt} - A_{jt-1} = \delta C_{jt} R_j + Mob_{jt} + \mu_j + \theta_{gt} + \nu_{jt}. \quad (3.3)$$

Third, we examined a subset of charter schools that has received relatively little attention in previous work: virtual schools. In Ohio, we examine whether virtual charter schools—which deliver services to students in their homes and enroll a substantial number of Ohio students—have different effects from those of classroom-based charter schools.

Finally, we examined the extent of variation in the performance of individual charter schools relative to individual TPSs. Most charter schools are single schools that are operated independently rather than under the authority of a larger organization, such as a school district. Moreover, one of the avowed purposes of charter-school laws is to promote diversity and innovation in educational options. As a consequence, we might expect wider variation in the performance of charter schools versus TPSs. We believe that this is the first study to examine empirically the variation in performance of charter schools and to compare it with the variation in performance of TPSs. To examine whether the performance of charter schools varies more than that of TPSs, we ran a regression in which we estimated an effect of each charter school and TPS in each location by creating a dummy variable for each individual charter school and TPS, then running a regression that created an estimate of each school, excluding one arbitrary school. We then compared the standard deviation of the average effect sizes of individual charter schools relative to the average effect sizes of individual TPSs.

For each location and corresponding data set included in our study, we had to make decisions about exclusions for various reasons, including incomplete test-score data for particular years or other anomalies. Appendix A provides a description of the data from each location and the decisions we made in terms of exclusions.

Notes on Interpreting Results

For simplicity, only the charter-related coefficients are presented in the tables of results that follow. More-detailed results can be found in Appendix B. Because all these analyses use fixed-effect models, all student characteristics that remain constant over time (while implicitly controlled for) are differenced out across all models. As a result, demographic characteristics, such as race and ethnicity, drop out of the models.

The coefficient estimates are presented in standardized effect sizes (i.e., units of standard deviations). These effect sizes are not easily translated into metrics, such as proportion of students achieving proficiency. But they can be compared with effects found in other studies using different tests. For example, researchers in education often cite the Tennessee class size–reduction study, in which effect sizes ranged from 0.15 to 0.25 (Krueger, 1999). Another policy-relevant comparison is the achievement gap between racial groups (C. Hill et al., 2007). In their analysis of National Assessment of Educational Progress (NAEP) scores, Hill and her colleagues found black-white achievement gaps of 0.67 to 0.83 in reading and 0.94 to 1.04 in math, depending on grade level. Hispanic-white achievement gaps ranged from 0.53 to 0.77 in reading and 0.68 to 0.85 in math.

We tested statistical significance at the standard 5-percent level and the more-stringent 1-percent level. We use both because our analysis includes a large number of tests of significance. By random chance, there is a possibility of falsely identifying an effect. Using a 1-percent level reduces this possibility.

Throughout the tables in this chapter, we present the results for the two statewide sites—Ohio and Texas—side by side following the results for the city-based sites. In both Ohio and Texas, we are using a statewide pool of students to standardize the test scores. In contrast, in the districts, we are using only districtwide data. Because this could have implications for the interpretation of effect sizes, we group our state results together and the district results together.

Initial Results. Table 3.1 presents the initial overall student achievement effect estimates in math and reading (in standardized units) as specified by Equation 3.1. In Ohio, Texas, and Chicago, the results apply only to elementary and middle-school grades because successive high-school grades are not included in our data in those sites. In a majority of cases, the results suggest that differences in the performance of charter schools and TPSs are small or nonexistent. In these cases, the gains of students attending charter schools are on par with the gains these same students experienced in TPSs. The only result that is positive and statistically significant at the 1-percent level is the math result in Denver, but caution is warranted in interpreting the Denver math results because the first three years of data in Denver include only a limited number of grades in which math was tested and because (as we will show later) the positive result is evident only in the first year of charter-school operation, which is directly contrary to patterns in other sites. Math results for two other sites (Ohio and Texas) are significantly

Table 3.1
Initial Math and Reading Student Achievement Effects, Averaged Across All Charter Schools in Each Jurisdiction

	Estimated Impact (robust standard error)	
Location	**Math Gains**	**Reading Gains**
Chicago	0.02 (0.02) *n* = 26	−0.04** (0.01) *n* = 26
Denver	0.17** (0.06) *n* = 21	0.04 (0.03) *n* = 21
Milwaukee	0.05* (0.02) *n* = 42	0.01 (0.01) *n* = 42
Philadelphia	−0.03 (0.02) *n* = 57	−0.03 (0.02) *n* = 57
San Diego	0.02 (0.02) *n* = 36	0.01 (0.01) *n* = 36
Ohio	−0.18** (0.04) *n* = 273	−0.08** (0.02) *n* = 271
Texas	−0.12** (0.02) *n* = 198	−0.08** (0.01) *n* = 198

NOTE: * = statistically significant at the 5-percent level. ** = statistically significant at the 1-percent level. *n* = number of charter schools included in the analysis.

negative. In reading, none of the results is significantly positive, and the results in Ohio and Texas are significantly negative.

In the pages that follow, we consider the interpretation of these results and possible threats to their validity, with a series of sensitivity tests and alternate analyses. We ultimately conclude that doubts are warranted about whether the results in Table 3.1 provide valid estimates of overall charter achievement effects, given the strong assumptions needed to estimate impacts for elementary schools (as well as other schools with kindergarten-entry grades, e.g., K–8 and K–12 schools).

We then present alternative analyses that produce estimates for which greater confidence is merited.

Sensitivity Tests

The results in Table 3.1 have two kinds of validity threats—those to internal validity and those to external validity. The results shown in Table 3.1 are internally valid if they are estimated without bias and, therefore, are reflective of the effects that charter schools have on the population included in the analysis—students who switch between TPSs and charter schools. The Table 3.1 results are externally valid if the results are reflective of the effect that charter schools have on charter students who are not included in the analysis—students who have test scores in charter schools but not in TPSs (*charter stayers*). There is no way to prove the internal and external validity of the results, but we can conduct sensitivity analyses to seek whether there is any clear evidence that the results are *not* internally or externally valid.

First, we address an internal validity threat. We examine whether the results in Table 3.1 might be biased by time-specific changes in achievement trajectories for transferring students (as suggested by Hoxby and Murarka, 2006). In Philadelphia and San Diego—the only sites with a sufficient number of grades and years included—we examined the math and reading achievement gains of transferring students immediately prior to attending charter schools. In particular, we examined whether the achievement gains of transferring students differed in the year immediately prior to transferring as compared with other years during which the student was enrolled in a TPS. This analysis was possible in Philadelphia and San Diego because our database of test results includes a large number of grades (2–10 in San Diego and, at maximum, 1–11 in Philadelphia) and a lengthy historical record (1997–98 through 2006–07 in San Diego and 2000–01 through 2006–07 in Philadelphia). As a result, we had the opportunity to observe students in TPSs and charter schools for a substantial number of years. In both sites and both subjects, students' achievement trajectories in the year immediately prior to transferring were indistinguishable from their trajectories in earlier years.[5] These results are consistent with a prior analysis of pretransfer achievement trajectories in Texas (Hanushek et al., 2005), and they do not suggest that pretransfer achievement dips would bias the impact estimates for Philadelphia and San Diego in Table 3.1.

Although the Philadelphia and San Diego (and previous Texas) results are encouraging from a methodological perspective, they can provide only limited support for the validity of the student fixed-effect analysis. Unfortunately, the data requirements of this analysis are onerous, and it cannot be conducted with any precision in sites other than Philadelphia and San Diego.[6] Assessing the distinctiveness of a future charter student's last year in a TPS prior to entering a charter school requires at least three years of test results before charter-school entry. When the band of consecutive grades tested is narrow, or when the historical data record is brief, few if any of the students transferring to charter schools have data meeting this requirement. In consequence, although we can have a reasonable level of confidence that pre-entry achievement dips are not substantially biasing results in Philadelphia and San Diego, we have no comparable information for any of the other sites. In five of seven sites, the existing empirical data cannot confirm or challenge the Hoxby/Murarka hypothesis regarding pretransfer changes in achievement trajectories. Some uncertainty therefore remains about the internal validity of the fixed-effect impact estimates in those sites.

A second internal validity threat relates to the reversibility assumption: Does the student switching out of a charter school provide information about the effectiveness of the prior charter school in the same way that a student switching into a charter school provides information about the effectiveness of the current charter school? In several of the locations, we ran alternative specifications that drew inferences

---

5 Point estimates suggested nonsignificant dips in achievement trajectories of 0.02 standard deviations in the pretransfer year in three of four comparisons; the fourth case (reading in Philadelphia) suggests a nonsignificant increase in the achievement trajectory in the pretransfer year of 0.01 standard deviations.

6 Our own data set in Texas, for example, includes a shorter historical panel than that used by Hanushek et al. (2005).

only from those switching in, ignoring those switching out. In some cases, the results differed from those in Table 3.1. These differences cast doubt on the validity of the reversibility assumption. This doubt is most problematic for charter elementary schools, in which kindergarten entrants provide none of the estimation power, and students leaving the school necessarily constitute a large proportion of those used to estimate impacts.

Third, we consider the possibility that the results in Table 3.1 could be externally invalid because they disproportionately weight schools that have more students switching between TPSs and charter schools (see Ballou, Teasley, and Zeidner, 2007). This could be particularly problematic if low-performing charter schools experience more student mobility than high-performing charter schools. To account for this possibility, we reweighted student observations (in five of the seven sites) to give each school a weight proportional to its enrollment.[7] The results were very similar to the results in Table 3.1, providing no evidence of bias from uneven representation.

To assess a related external validity threat, we examine whether the annual achievement gains of transferring students (on whom the estimates in Table 3.1 are based) are representative of the larger population of charter students (also noted by Hoxby and Murarka as a potential problem). We compare the average annual achievement gains of transferring students—across all years of their enrollment, in TPSs as well as charter schools—to the average annual achievement gains of students who are observed only in a charter school (charter stayers), and we examine the relative proportions of switchers and stayers among all charter students in our data.[8] The percentage of students who are switchers is a function not only of the mobility of the charter schools' populations, but also of the number of grades tested, the grade configurations of the charter schools, and the number of years of data available to us.

---

7 We were unable to run this sensitivity analysis in Ohio and Texas because of the computational time required to run these models in these locations.

8 For the analysis, we also include school fixed effects to control for between-school differences.

The results in Table 3.2 indicate that, in just over half of the comparisons, students observed only in charter schools have gains that are not statistically different (at 0.05) from students who switch between charter and TPS status. But charter stayers have significantly (at 0.05 and usually at 0.01) larger gains in nearly half of the comparisons, including Ohio and Texas, where the achievement estimates were negative in Table 3.1.

The larger average gains for charter stayers (versus switchers) are not surprising: Staying in one school may be an indication of family stability, and switching schools may occur because a student has not been doing well in the prior school. Whether these differences create an

Table 3.2
Descriptive Student Achievement Gains for Students Always in Charter Schools Relative to Students Who Transfer Between Charter Schools and Traditional Public Schools

Location	Percentage of Charter Students Observed Switching Between TPSs and Charter Schools	Average Annual Gain Advantage for Students Always in Charter Schools Versus Students Who Transfer (robust standard error)	
		Math	Reading
Chicago	43.3	0.03* (0.01)	0.02 (0.01)
Denver	47.3	0.03 (0.05)	0.03 (0.04)
Milwaukee	73.6	–0.01 (0.02)	0.01 (0.01)
Philadelphia	57.0	0.03** (0.01)	0.01 (0.01)
San Diego	73.7	0.00 (0.02)	0.00 (0.02)
Ohio	47.4	0.09** (0.03)	0.06** (0.02)
Texas	71.3	0.16** (0.02)	0.10** (0.01)

NOTE: * = statistically significant at the 5-percent level. ** = statistically significant at the 1-percent level.

external validity threat to the results in Table 3.1 is unclear: It is possible that charter schools have similar effects on stayers and switchers even though the two groups have different overall achievement trajectories. Nevertheless, the underlying differences cast doubt on the assumption that the effects are the same across the two groups. We do not know whether charter stayers experience different effects than charter switchers do, and we cannot be sure that they experience the same effects.

The fact that we cannot estimate impacts for charter students who never attend TPSs is problematic primarily for assessing charter elementary schools. Effects for elementary charters are assessed based on changes in the performance trajectories of two groups of students: those who transfer into the charter schools late, after they have already been enrolled in TPSs long enough to complete at least two tested grades, and those who transfer out of the charter schools and into TPSs. The first group may be unusual simply because its members chose to transfer midstream. The second group may not be unusual, but using it to estimate impacts relies on the reversibility assumption, which may not be valid. Indeed, the difficulty of estimating impacts for charter elementary schools is serious enough that a recent report on Boston charter schools (Abdulkadiroglu et al., 2009) omitted elementary charters entirely.

For charter schools that begin at higher grade levels, in contrast to those that begin in kindergarten, all students had to transfer in, so the estimates of the impacts of the schools are not based on an unusual subsample of transfer students.[9] Moreover, a necessarily higher proportion of the switching students are those who transfer into charter schools rather than transferring out, reducing the reliance on the reversibility assumption. We therefore conducted an alternative analysis that included only the subset of charter schools with entry grades that are high enough to allow us to measure gain scores in TPSs prior to entry.[10]

---

[9] This analysis is nonetheless not quite comprehensive because it excludes students who transferred from a charter elementary or private school.

[10] For instance, in San Diego, the lowest grade tested in math and reading is second grade. Therefore, to be included in the analysis, a student must attend a charter school with a lowest

In these schools, which we label *nonprimary charter schools*, stayers as well as off-grade switchers contribute to the impact estimates.

Narrowing the analysis to include only charter schools with entry grades high enough to allow pretreatment gain calculations for entering students means that charter elementary schools (as well as K–8 and K–12 charter schools)—which represent a large proportion of all charter schools in most of our locations—are excluded from the analysis. Differences between the results for nonprimary schools and the results in Table 3.1 for all charter schools might indicate bias in the results shown in Table 3.1 or might simply indicate that elementary charter schools have different effects than do charter schools with higher entry grades (i.e., middle schools, high schools, and combination middle-high schools). Either way, we have more confidence in the results for nonprimary charter schools than in the results in Table 3.1.

Table 3.3 presents estimated impacts for nonprimary charter schools in each of the sites. Of the 14 estimates across the seven locales, 11 suggest charter-school impacts that are indistinguishable from those of TPSs. Three of the estimates are significantly negative, for middle schools in Chicago in reading (at 0.01) and middle schools in Texas in both subjects (at 0.01 in reading and 0.05 in math). High schools are not included in this analysis in Chicago and Texas because test data are unavailable in successive high-school grades in those sites. (Chicago's high schools are analyzed using a different method in Chapter Four.)

Interestingly, the results for nonprimary schools in Table 3.3 for many of the sites are quite consistent with the results in Table 3.1 that included elementary schools. All of the results that are statistically indistinguishable from 0 in Table 3.1 remain so in Table 3.3. In Milwaukee, the small positive result in math in Table 3.1 declines slightly and loses statistical significance in Table 3.3, but the point estimate does not change much. Similarly, Denver's positive math effect reduces in magnitude and becomes statistically insignificant. The significantly

grade of at least fourth grade. Because the grades tested changed over time for some locations, the lowest grade varies by year.

Table 3.3
Estimated Impacts of Nonprimary Charter Schools

	Estimated Impact (robust standard error)	
Location	**Math Gains**	**Reading Gains**
Chicago	−0.06 (0.04) *n* = 6	−0.09** (0.02) *n* = 6
Denver	0.10 (0.06) *n* = 12	0.03 (0.03) *n* = 12
Milwaukee	0.03 (0.02) *n* = 30	0.00 (0.01) *n* = 32
Philadelphia	−0.02 (0.03) *n* = 26	0.00 (0.02) *n* = 26
San Diego	0.01 (0.02) *n* = 18	0.02 (0.02) *n* = 18
Ohio	−0.01 (0.07) *n* = 62	0.00 (0.05) *n* = 56
Texas	−0.08* (0.04) *n* = 75	−0.08** (0.02) *n* = 75

NOTE: * = statistically significant at the 5-percent level. ** = statistically significant at the 1-percent level. *n* = number of charter schools included in the analysis.

negative results in Chicago (reading) and Texas (both subjects) remain significantly negative in Table 3.3.

Ohio, however, presents a different story. The substantial negative results suggested in Table 3.1 disappear when focusing on the subset of nonprimary charter schools. For Ohio's charter middle schools (our test data in Ohio end at eighth grade, so high schools are not included), estimated achievement impacts are indistinguishable from those of TPSs. We examine the differences in the Ohio results more closely in the next section of this chapter.

The largely corresponding results in Tables 3.1 and 3.3 are encouraging: The correspondence is consistent with the possibility that the estimates in Table 3.1 (except in Ohio) are valid across grade levels, i.e., for the full universe of charter schools in each site. But mere correspondence cannot confirm the validity of the results in Table 3.1. Reasons for doubting their validity as applied to elementary charter schools include the differences between switchers and nonswitchers in descriptive achievement gains, the absence of information on the baseline achievement trajectories of students who enroll in charter schools starting in kindergarten, and the disproportionate reliance on the reversibility assumption. In consequence, we suggest great caution in interpreting the results of Table 3.1. The estimates from Table 3.1 for Ohio are especially doubtful.

The results for nonprimary schools in Table 3.3 are, in all sites, less susceptible to the biases just identified. Those results suggest that the performance of nonprimary charter schools is approximately on par with that of TPSs in most of the sites, though middle schools in Texas and Chicago appear to be falling behind.

Student Achievement in Virtual Charter Schools

Assessing the dramatic differences in Ohio's results in Table 3.1 versus those in Table 3.3 requires attention to virtual charter schools—also known as electronic schools, e-schools, cyber charters, or non–classroom-based charters—which deliver education to students in their own homes, using such technologies as home computers, the Internet, and telephone support. Ohio is one of several states (also including Pennsylvania and California) where virtual charter schools have been especially prominent and especially controversial. Virtual charters have been the subject of suspicion for both financial reasons and performance reasons. For instance, in California, a previous RAND report found that non–classroom-based charter schools exhibited lower test scores than TPSs or other types of charter schools, controlling for observable student characteristics (Zimmer, Buddin, et al., 2003). In addition, concerns have been raised about how public resources were being used within these schools, leading California policymakers to establish greater financial oversight. Similar concerns have been expressed in

Ohio, resulting in a moratorium on the establishment of new virtual schools in the state.

Despite the moratorium, Ohio data include a large-enough sample of virtual charter schools to permit a comparison of the performance of the virtual and classroom-based charter schools. As many as 40 virtual charter schools have operated in Ohio. In the 2008–09 school year, 34 of Ohio's 328 charter schools were virtual charter schools, serving approximately 22 percent of charter students statewide. Table 3.4 displays the results of student fixed-effect achievement analyses for virtual charter schools versus classroom-based charter schools in Ohio. The estimates for the virtual charter schools are negative, substantial, and (in three of four estimates) statistically significant. In contrast, all estimates for nonvirtual schools are close to 0 and not statistically significant. When we limit the analysis to nonprimary charter schools (which, in Ohio's data, means middle schools), the impact estimates are almost unchanged: Virtual charter middle schools lag substantially

Table 3.4
Estimated Math and Reading Student Achievement Impacts in Virtual and Classroom-Based Charter Schools in Ohio

	Estimated Impact (robust standard error)	
Variable	**Math**	**Reading**
Attending a virtual charter school, all grades	−0.44** (0.04) *n* = 39	−0.25** (0.03) *n* = 40
Attending a classroom-based charter school, all grades	−0.05 (0.03) *n* = 239	−0.01 (0.02) *n* = 236
Attending a nonprimary virtual charter school	−0.65* (0.25) *n* = 4	−0.13 (0.24) *n* = 3
Attending a nonprimary classroom-based charter school	0.00 (0.06) *n* = 59	0.00 (0.05) *n* = 54

NOTE: * = statistically significant at the 5-percent level. ** = statistically significant at the 1-percent level. *n* = number of virtual and classroom-based charter schools included in the analysis.

behind classroom-based charter middle schools (which show effects comparable to those of conventional middle schools). In short, the large negative estimates seen in Table 3.1 are almost entirely attributable to virtual charter schools, the great majority of which begin in kindergarten and therefore drop out of Table 3.3.

Despite the consistency of the negative results for Ohio's virtual charter schools, caution is warranted in interpretation. Many of the students attending these schools do not contribute to the impact estimates, either because they entered the virtual school in kindergarten or because they were previously homeschooled. These students would not be captured in this analysis because they never switched status between a charter school and a TPS. Moreover, the switchers who contribute to the estimated impacts may be students who are especially likely to have experienced an event producing a decline in their expected future achievement: The decision to exit a TPS in favor of a home-based educational setting can, in many cases, signal that the student was heading for significant problems in the TPS. In addition, examining the achievement gains of switchers versus stayers, we found significant differences. Stayers have higher achievement gains of 0.28 and 0.20 of a standard deviation in math and reading. Together, these issues suggest some uncertainty in the causal and external validity of the impact estimates for virtual charter schools, but the size of the estimated achievement declines for enrolled students nonetheless merits concern.

Student Achievement, by Age of Charter School

Reform efforts require time to take hold and have an effect. For instance, researchers on comprehensive school reform have demonstrated a positive relationship between length of implementation and student achievement (Slavin et al., 1994; Ross, Nunnery, and Smith, 1996; Catterall, 1995). Ross, Sanders, et al. (2001, p. 327) note that "leading scholars of educational change have hypothesized that finding measurable results will, at best, take between 3 and 10 years" (see also Fullan and Stiegelbauer, 1991; Fullan, 1999; Fullan and Miles, 1992). Similarly, researchers and comprehensive school reform–model developers have pointed out that it may take more than five years to accomplish meaningful schoolwide change (Sizer, 1992; G. Hess, 1995; Darling-Hammond, 1988, 1995, 1997).

Charter schools may likewise take time to achieve peak effectiveness. In this section, we examine the extent to which the estimated achievement impact of charter schools changes as the schools gain more experience. Again, this analysis relies on student fixed effects, which identify impacts by comparing the achievement gains of individual students with their own achievement gains in other years. However, for this analysis, we are most interested in examining differences in performance from the first year of operation to the third or more years of operation. For the first year of operation, the estimate would be based on switchers. For the second- and third-year estimates, much of the estimates would be driven by these students who switched into the charter school in the initial year, a fact that should allow us to gain insights into the pattern of achievement over time.

Table 3.5 presents the results from Equation 3.2 for students attending a charter school in operation for one, two, or three or more years. One could argue that the results for charter schools that have been around for three or more years should be our primary results if policymakers are most interested in the long-term outcomes of charter

Table 3.5
Estimates for Math and Reading Student Achievement While Attending a Charter School, by Age of Charter School

Year of Charter School's Operation	Coefficient (robust standard error)	
	Math	**Reading**
Chicago		
First	−0.24** (0.06) *n* = 6	−0.11** (0.02) *n* = 6
Second	−0.04 (0.05) *n* = 17	−0.04 (0.03) *n* = 17
Third or more	0.06** (0.01) *n* = 19	−0.03 (0.01) *n* = 19

Table 3.5—Continued

Year of Charter School's Operation	Coefficient (robust standard error)	
	Math	Reading
Denver		
First	0.25* (0.10) n = 12	0.01 (0.04) n = 12
Second	0.13 (0.13) n = 12	0.03 (0.04) n = 12
Third or more	0.16 (0.09) n = 14	0.05 (0.04) n = 14
Milwaukee		
First	−0.02 (0.04) n = 38	0.00 (0.02) n = 38
Second	0.04 (0.04) n = 30	−0.01 (0.02) n = 30
Third or more	0.05 (0.03) n = 20	0.01 (0.01) n = 20
Philadelphia		
First	−0.01 (0.08) n = 22	0.02 (0.05) n = 22
Second	−0.01 (0.04) n = 29	−0.04 (0.03) n = 29
Third or more	−0.04 (0.02) n = 52	−0.03 (0.02) n = 52

Table 3.5—Continued

Year of Charter School's Operation	Coefficient (robust standard error)	
	Math	Reading
San Diego		
First	0.01 (0.08) n = 29	0.00 (0.03) n = 29
Second	0.02 (0.05) n = 27	0.01 (0.02) n = 27
Third or more	0.02 (0.02) n = 22	0.02 (0.02) n = 22
Ohio		
First	–0.30** (0.12) n = 54	–0.17 (0.09) n = 80
Second	–0.23** (0.06) n = 115	–0.13* (0.04) n = 125
Third or more	–0.17** (0.04) n = 227	–0.07* (0.03) n = 226
Texas		
First	–0.22** (0.04) n = 133	–0.14** (0.03) n = 133
Second	–0.10** (0.03) n = 142	–0.11** (0.02) n = 142
Third or more	–0.08** (0.02) n = 148	–0.04** (0.01) n = 148

NOTE: * = statistically significant at the 5-percent level. ** = statistically significant at the 1-percent level. n = number of charter schools included in the analysis.

schools, realizing that there may be some transition issues. However, relying on the estimated effects of schools that have been in place for three or more years has three drawbacks. First, the effects for charter schools that have been in operation three or more years do not present a comprehensive picture of *all* charter schools because many charter schools have not reached their third year of operation. Second, because of poor performance, some charter schools may not reach the third year of operation and shut down. An evaluation that focuses entirely on the third year of performance would not capture the results for these schools. Third, and finally, policymakers created charter-school laws with the intention of spawning new schools; newness is therefore an inherent part of the charter treatment.

Table 3.5 reinforces findings from previous studies suggesting that the first year of operation is often a difficult one for charter schools. Across the seven sites, five out of 14 first-year impact estimates are significantly negative, while only one is significantly positive; the rest are indistinguishable from 0. In addition, there is a general pattern of coefficients improving over time: In 10 of 14 subject-site combinations, point estimates for impacts after three or more years of operation are superior to estimates for first-year charter schools. Nonetheless, it is not clear that this improvement systematically leads to producing charter schools that are more effective than TPSs. In only one case (Chicago in math) is the impact estimate for three or more years positive and statistically significant. So although the coefficient estimates often point to improvement over time, they generally do not reach a result that exceeds the effects of TPSs by a statistically significant margin. The sites where charter schools show the largest improvements in performance as they gain experience are Chicago, Ohio, and Texas, where the average effects for first-year charter schools are substantially negative; subsequent improvement in Ohio and Texas merely makes the results less negative. Only the math estimate for Chicago charter schools shifts from significantly negative to significantly positive as the charter schools gain experience.

Student Achievement, by Race

Given the challenges in estimating the effects of elementary charter schools, we examine differential outcomes by race only in the subset of charter schools (i.e., nonprimary charters) that are included in Table 3.3. As shown in Table 3.6, most of the analyses by race show no statistically significant effects one way or the other. There are some exceptions, but the exceptions show no clear patterns across sites, with positive and negative effects estimated for each racial group in different locations.

Table 3.6
Estimates for Math and Reading Student Achievement Effects, by Race or Ethnicity, Nonprimary Charter Schools

	Coefficient (robust standard error)	
Variable	**Math**	**Reading**
Chicago		
African American	0.02 (0.03)	−0.04 (0.03)
Hispanic	−0.14** (0.04)	−0.14** (0.02)
White	−0.08 (0.13)	−0.09 (0.08)
Denver		
African American	0.13 (0.08)	0.01 (0.05)
Hispanic	0.07 (0.07)	0.05 (0.03)
White	0.23** (0.06)	−0.08 (0.07)
Milwaukee		
African American	0.02 (0.02)	0.00 (0.01)
Hispanic	0.05 (0.03)	0.00 (0.02)

Table 3.6—Continued

	Coefficient (robust standard error)	
Variable	**Math**	**Reading**
White	0.03 (0.03)	0.03 (0.02)
Philadelphia		
African American	–0.04 (0.03)	–0.01 (0.03)
Hispanic	0.04 (0.04)	0.02 (0.02)
White	0.04 (0.03)	0.03 (0.03)
San Diego		
African American	0.05 (0.03)	0.05** (0.01)
Hispanic	0.00 (0.04)	0.01 (0.02)
White	0.01 (0.03)	0.03 (0.03)
Ohio		
African American	0.06 (0.09)	0.04 (0.07)
Hispanic	0.08 (0.21)	–0.13 (0.13)
White	–0.10 (0.07)	0.01 (0.07)
Texas		
African American	–0.03 (0.06)	–0.08* (0.04)
Hispanic	–0.10* (0.05)	–0.08* (0.03)
White	–0.14** (0.04)	–0.10* (0.04)

NOTE: * = statistically significant at the 5-percent level. ** = statistically significant at the 1-percent level.

Examination of the Variance in Performance

Finally, we examined whether charter schools vary more than TPSs in performance, as measured by the estimated achievement impact of each individual school in each of our locations. This involved running a regression in which each individual school is included as a dummy variable (excluding a single, arbitrary school, against which the performance of each of the dummied schools is implicitly compared). This analysis relies on the same student fixed-effect approach as does the analysis in Table 3.1. The impact estimates for individual schools would be subject to the same methodological concerns that raise questions for the results in Table 3.1, but we do not expect that any biases in those estimates for individual schools would, in the aggregate, differ for charter schools versus TPSs. If these biases for individual school estimates are comparable in charter schools and TPSs, then the comparison of the range of performance in the two types of schools should be unbiased.

To avoid having the results skewed by very small schools, we excluded any school that had fewer than 10 measured student achievement gains. We also conducted a sensitivity analysis excluding any school with fewer than 100 measured student achievement gains. The sensitivity analysis eliminates a large number of schools, but the results were similar to the patterns seen with the 10-student restriction, with no changes to the substantive conclusions. After calculating the estimates for each individual school, we compared the standard deviation of the average achievement effect of charter schools relative to the standard deviation of the average achievement effect of TPSs. These results are presented in Table 3.7.[11]

In most of the locations, charter schools have slightly greater variance than TPSs in estimated achievement impact. The differences

---

[11] To test whether the standard deviations are significantly different between the two groups, we used Bartlett's test and Levene's robust test statistic for the equality of variances. (In Stata, the commands for these tests are sdtest and robvar, respectively.) We used both tests because the Bartlett test, while more straightforward, can be sensitive to the underlying assumptions of the distribution of the data, while Levene's robust test statistic for the equality of variances is more robust under nonnormal distribution of data (Levene, 1960). Across the locations, the tests produced the same results in assessing differences in variance.

Table 3.7
Standard Deviations of School-Level Achievement Effects, Charter and Traditional Public Schools

	Math		Reading	
Location	**Charter**	**TPS**	**Charter**	**TPS**
Chicago	0.14*	0.10*	0.11	0.10
Denver	0.26	0.21	0.14	0.12
Milwaukee	0.22	0.22	0.13	0.17
Philadelphia	0.20	0.19	0.11*	0.15*
San Diego	0.22*	0.15*	0.16*	0.11*
Ohio	0.51*	0.31*	0.58*	0.32*
Texas	0.34*	0.28*	0.30*	0.25*

NOTE: * = statistically significant at the 5-percent level.

in variance often achieve statistical significance, but they are small in most sites, with the notable exception of Ohio. Indeed, except in Ohio, it is not clear that the differences in variance are any greater than would be expected to result from greater measurement error associated with the smaller average size of charter schools. Even in the sensitivity analysis that excludes all schools with fewer than 100 student gain measures, the remaining charter schools have, on average, fewer students contributing to impact estimates than do the remaining TPSs. At either threshold, in most sites, the variation in the estimated performance of charter schools is only marginally greater than the variation in the estimated performance of TPSs.

The substantially greater variance in the performance of charter schools in Ohio, by contrast, cannot easily be explained away. When we restrict attention to schools with more than 100 student gains, Ohio's charter schools still have greater variance in performance than its TPSs—despite the fact that, at this threshold, the average size of charter schools in Ohio is larger than the average size of TPSs.[12] Moreover, the large variance in the performance of Ohio charters is not primarily attributable to the virtual schools: The differences in standard deviations between TPSs and charter schools in Ohio are similar if we exclude virtual schools.

Chapter Summary

In this chapter, we estimated the achievement impacts of charter schools by examining the achievement gains of students while attending charter schools relative to the gains the same students experience in a TPS. We conducted a number of sensitivity analyses to assess whether there is evidence that our results may be internally or externally invalid. We find greater reason for concern about the validity of the results for charter schools with primary grades, because prekindergarten test scores are unavailable for students in those schools and because estimates for those schools must rely disproportionately on the assumption that their effects are measurable based on changes in the achievement trajectories of their students after they leave the schools. We therefore have greater confidence in our estimates for the effects of nonprimary charter schools, where most students have pretreatment test scores that can be used to derive the estimates.

The analysis suggests that nonprimary charter schools are producing achievement gains that are approximately equivalent to those of TPSs in most locations, with moderately negative effects in math and reading in Texas middle schools and in reading in Chicago middle schools. While our results for Ohio's virtual charter schools should be viewed with a level of caution because of the uniqueness of the students who attend these schools and because much of the analysis relies on charter schools with primary grades, they suggest that these schools should be examined more carefully because of the poor achievement

---

[12] Among the Ohio schools with at least 100 student gain measures, the standard deviations of the impact estimates in reading are 0.44 for charters and 0.28 for TPSs and in math are 0.31 for charters and 0.24 for TPSs.

results. We find support for the conclusion that, in most locations, charter schools do not do well in their first year of operation but subsequently improve (though sometimes this improvement is sufficient only to produce a result that is somewhat less negative than in the first year of operation). Finally, we find that charter schools in most locales have marginally greater variation in performance than TPSs, as measured by the achievement-impact estimate for each school. Ohio is a notable exception: Its charter schools have a much wider range of variation in performance than its TPSs.

CHAPTER FOUR

Educational Attainment Effects of Charter High Schools

So far, this monograph has focused on test scores as a measure of charter-school effectiveness. However, test scores are really only proxies for learning and for outcomes that students, parents, educators, policymakers, and society as a whole care more about, such as graduation and college enrollment. Despite the interest in these outcomes, researchers evaluating charter-school impacts have generally not focused on these measures as outcomes.[1] The absence of such research has been due partly to the absence of data, as most districts and states do not have reliable graduation data or have not linked K–12 data to postsecondary data.

Even when these data are available, the analysis can be complicated, especially in the context of programs or schools that students choose to attend. As noted previously, when examining charter schools as an option in which students can choose to participate, researchers worry that these students may be different in ways that are not readily observable from those who choose to attend TPSs. The fact that the charter students and their parents actively sought out an alternative to TPSs suggests that the students may be more motivated or their parents may be more involved in their child's education than are the families of TPS attendees. Since these traits are not readily observable, they could be falsely attributed to the charter schools and thus bias the estimate of the impact of charter schools.

[1] Indeed, the only study of charter schools we have seen that attempts to assess impacts on attainment is a small study of a single school in San Diego (McClure et al., 2005).

Previously, we used a fixed-effect approach as a way of controlling for the selection bias. This approach, however, is applicable only to situations in which there are repeated outcome measures over time for a single student. Assuming that student and family characteristics are constant over time, the variation in test scores for students who move between TPSs and charters can be used to infer the differential impacts of the two types of schools on student achievement while holding student and family characteristics constant. However, since only a single outcome is observed in the present context (e.g., a student receives a high-school diploma or not), the fixed-effect approach cannot be used. We therefore require another approach to address selection bias in assessing the impact of charter schools on the probability of graduating from high school and attending college.

We employ three methods to deal with the selection-bias problem. The first strategy is to control for any observable differences in charter and noncharter high-school students prior to high-school entry. These include such factors as race and ethnicity, gender, disability status, and family income. Most important among these are eighth-grade test scores, to capture differences in student ability and past educational inputs received prior to high school.

The second strategy for dealing with selection bias is to focus on students who attended a charter school in grade 8, just prior to beginning high school. If there are unmeasured student or family characteristics that lead to the selection of charter high schools, these unmeasured characteristics ought to also lead to the choice of a charter school at the middle-school level. Thus, comparisons of TPS eighth graders and charter-school eighth graders would likely be biased due to self-selection. The unobserved student and family characteristics should be relatively constant within the subgroup of charter eighth graders, however. This is the same approach that Altonji, Elder, and Taber (2005) take in the context of evaluating Catholic high schools. We believe that this restriction is critical for internal validity, but we acknowledge that it involves an external validity trade-off: Charter–high school students who did not attend charter middle schools are not included in the analysis, and it is possible that charter schools have different effects on those students.

The third strategy for addressing selection bias follows Neal (1997) and Grogger and Neal (2000) in their analyses of Catholic high schools. We exploit variation in the location of charter high schools to construct instruments for the choice of attending a charter high school. For many charter–middle school students, attending a charter high school may be infeasible due to the unavailability of a charter high school within a reasonable distance.

Data

The data required to analyze the impact of charter high schools on educational attainment are substantial. One must have data on school type and educational outcomes of individual students prior to high school, individual-level high-school attendance and exit information, and data on college attendance after high school. On top of this, the jurisdiction studied must have a sufficient enrollment of students in charter high schools to provide reliable results. The areas we analyze, the state of Florida and the city of Chicago, are two of perhaps a handful of places where all of the necessary data elements are currently in place. (For more information on the data in both Chicago and Florida, see Appendix A.)

In Florida, high-school graduation is determined by withdrawal information and student-award data from the K–20 Education Data Warehouse (EDW). Only students who receive a standard high-school diploma are considered to be high-school graduates. Students earning a General Educational Development Test (GED®) or special-education diploma are counted as not graduating. Similarly, students who withdrew with no intention of returning or exited for other reasons, such as nonattendance, court action, joining the military, marriage, pregnancy, and medical problems, but did not later graduate are counted as not graduating. Students who died while in school are removed from the sample. It is not possible to directly determine the graduation status of students who leave the Florida public school system to attend a homeschooling program or to enroll in a private school or who move out of state. Similarly, some students leave the public school system for unknown reasons. Students whose graduation status is unknown are more likely to have lower eighth-grade test scores and possess other characteristics associated with a reduced likelihood of graduation.[2] They also are more likely to initially attend a traditional high school rather than a charter high school. To avoid possible bias associated with differential sample attrition, we impute the graduation status for those students whose graduation outcome is unknown, based on predicted values from a regression model of graduation.[3] Since we can track college attendance both within and outside of Florida, no imputation is necessary for the college-attendance variable. Any individual who does not show up as enrolled in a two-year or four-year college or university is classified as a nonattendee.

The available data in Florida cover four cohorts of eighth-grade students. Statewide achievement testing for eighth-grade students began in the 1997–98 school year, so the first cohort in the sample is students who attended eighth grade in 1997–98.[4] The last available year of student data is 2004–05. Given that high-school completion typically takes four years, this means that the last cohort that can be tracked through high school is students who attended grade 8 in 2000–01.

In Chicago, high-school graduation is determined by withdrawal information from Chicago Public Schools data. Only students who

---

2 Sample attrition in Florida is 22 percent for charter-to-traditional students and only 15 percent for charter-to-charter students. In Chicago, the numbers are reversed: 13-percent attrition in the charter-to-traditional sample and 20 percent in the charter-to-charter sample.

3 Imputation was done with the uvis procedure in Stata. All variables reported in Table 4.2, except for the charter–high school attendance variable, were used to predict graduation. Since imputation is based on observable factors, it does not account for unmeasured student characteristics that may be correlated with both sample attrition and high-school graduation. Therefore, our imputation method may not completely eliminate attrition bias. If students whose graduation status is unknown are removed from the sample (rather than having their graduation status imputed), we obtain similar, though somewhat larger, estimated effects of charter attendance on high-school graduation. See Tables 4.8 and 4.9.

4 Data on limited English proficiency (LEP) and special education–program participation begin in 1998–99 and are thus not available for the first eighth-grade cohort. For these students, we use the LEP and special-education status in ninth grade.

receive a standard high-school diploma are considered to be high-school graduates. For students who leave the Chicago public school system, we impute their graduation status with a regression model as described for Florida. For Chicago, we have college attendance data only for students who graduated from the Chicago public school system, so we also impute college attendance for students with missing graduation data, using the same regression model as for graduation imputation.

From 1998–99 through 2001–02, the number of charter schools in Florida with high-school grades grew from 19 to 44. In contrast, from 1998–99 through 2002–03, the number of Chicago charter schools with high-school grades increased only from six to seven. Of the seven Chicago charter high schools in operation in 2002–03, six had nontraditional configurations that encompassed grades prior to ninth grade. In contrast, 26 of the 36 charter schools with high-school grades in Florida had a traditional grade configuration of grades 9 through 12.

Results

Summary statistics on educational attainment are provided in Table 4.1. For each jurisdiction, the students are broken down by transition type: charter middle school to traditional public high school and charter middle school to charter high school.[5] The full sample includes more than 5,000 students: more than 4,200 students from Florida and nearly 1,000 students from Chicago.

The raw data reveal substantial differences in educational attainment between charter and traditional public high-school attendees. In Florida, 57 percent of students who went from a charter school in

---

[5] Throughout the analysis, exposure to a charter high school is defined by the type of school a student attends in grade 9 and whether he or she subsequently stays in that type of school. As illustrated in Table C.1 in Appendix C, significant numbers of students switch school types (primarily from charters back to TPSs) after ninth grade. Excluding these students has little effect on the results, however (see Tables C.2 and C.3). Nonetheless, the estimates of charter-school effects should be interpreted as an "attempt to treat."

Table 4.1
Descriptive Statistics, by Transition Type

	Florida				Chicago			
	Charter in G8, TPS in G9		Charter in G8 and in G9		Charter in G8, TPS in G9		Charter in G8 and in G9	
Variable	**Obs.**	**Mean**	**Obs.**	**Mean**	**Obs.**	**Mean**	**Obs.**	**Mean**
Any college in 5 yrs.	1,526	0.402	572	0.556	295	0.383	299	0.488
4-yr. college in 5	1,523	0.148	570	0.305				
HS diploma in 4	2,149	0.571	1,066	0.795				
HS diploma in 4 (with imputation)	2,762	0.567	1,259	0.770				
HS diploma in 5	1,123	0.568	460	0.783				
HS diploma in 5 (with imputation)	1,445	0.566	551	0.764				
HS diploma ever					456	0.678	381	0.753
HS diploma ever (with imputation)					523	0.597	474	0.636
Math score, G8	2,831	291.258	1,293	310.083	517	246.342	471	236.896
Reading score, G8	2,818	283.195	1,283	300.984	515	240.309	471	232.406
Female	2,914	0.467	1,304	0.486	523	0.53	474	0.563
African American	2,893	0.370	1,295	0.178	523	0.834	474	0.835

Table 4.1—Continued

	Florida				Chicago			
	Charter in G8, TPS in G9		Charter in G8 and in G9		Charter in G8, TPS in G9		Charter in G8 and in G9	
Variable	Obs.	Mean	Obs.	Mean	Obs.	Mean	Obs.	Mean
Hispanic	2,893	0.106	1,295	0.189	523	0.132	474	0.143
Asian	2,893	0.010	1,295	0.017	523	0.002	474	0
LEP/bilingual in G8	2,914	0.009	1,304	0.023	523	0.082	474	0.093
Special ed in G8	2,914	0.152	1,304	0.103	523	0.134	474	0.108
Free/reduced-price lunch in G8	2,914	0.411	1,304	0.225	463	0.896	395	0.896
Change schools in G7–8	2,663	0.674	1,175	0.716	523	0.264	474	0.272
1997 G8 cohort	2,914	0.027	1,304	0.001				
1998 G8 cohort	2,914	0.115	1,304	0.102	523	0.061	474	0.114
1999 G8 cohort	2,914	0.382	1,304	0.336	523	0.153	474	0.19
2000 G8 cohort	2,914	0.476	1,304	0.561	523	0.203	474	0.177
2001 G8 cohort					523	0.231	474	0.306
2002 G8 cohort					523	0.352	474	0.213

grade 8 to a traditional public school in grade 9 received a standard high-school diploma within four years, whereas 77 percent of students attending a charter school in grade 9 earned their diplomas within four years. In Chicago, 68 percent of charter–middle school students who transitioned to a TPS in grade 9 eventually received their high-school diplomas, whereas 75 percent of students who transitioned to a charter high school received their diplomas. Similar differentials are found for college attendance as well. In Florida, 57 percent of students attending a charter school in grade 9 went to either a two-year or four-year post-secondary institution within five years of starting high school, whereas, among students who started high school in a TPS, the college attendance rate was only 40 percent. In Chicago, the gap in college attendance is smaller but still sizable: 49 percent for charter–high school attendees and 38 percent for charter–middle school students who go to a traditional public high school.

Probit Estimates of the Determinants of Educational Attainment

While the descriptive results provide initial insights into the differences in graduation and college-attendance rates between charter and traditional public high schools, we also examine these differences using a probit analysis that simultaneously assesses the contribution of multiple student characteristics in predicting the probability that a student graduates or enrolls in college. This approach is often used when examining dichotomous outcomes (Maddala, 1983). We conduct separate probit analyses for the two outcome measures of graduating and enrolling in college. The independent variables describe the relationship between the student characteristics and the probability of graduating or enrolling in college.

Tables 4.2 and 4.3 contain the probit estimates of the determinants of high-school graduation and college attendance, respectively. The interpretation of raw output of the model is complicated somewhat by the fact that the coefficients reflect changes in standard deviations. Because thinking of relationships in terms of standard deviations can be difficult, we convert the coefficient outcomes into changes in probabilities at the mean values for continuous variables and the change from 0 to 1 for discrete variables. To better illustrate the meaning of

Table 4.2
Probit Estimates of Receiving a Standard High-School Diploma (coefficient estimates are marginal effects)

	Florida		Chicago
Variable	**Within 4 Years**	**Within 5 Years**	**Within 5+ Years**
Attend charter HS	0.1223*** (0.0318)	0.1481*** (0.0375)	0.0741** (0.0376)
Math score, G8	0.0033*** (0.0003)	0.0034*** (0.0004)	0.0016** (0.0008)
Reading score, G8	0.0021*** (0.0002)	0.0018*** (0.0003)	0.0023*** (0.0007)
Female	0.0678*** (0.0159)	0.0474* (0.0268)	0.0682** (0.0331)
African American	0.0559*** (0.0202)	0.1062*** (0.0329)	0.1961** (0.0928)
Hispanic	0.0912*** (0.0275)	0.1184** (0.0445)	0.0875 (0.1080)
Asian	0.0993 (0.0864)	0.1446 (0.1100)	
LEP/bilingual, G8	0.0628 (0.0956)	0.1192 (0.1345)	−0.0070 (0.0890)
Special ed, G8	0.0931*** (0.0309)	0.0792** (0.0379)	0.0846* (0.0450)
Free/reduced-price lunch, G8	−0.1718*** (0.0240)	−0.1300*** (0.0329)	−0.0292 (0.0636)
Changed schools, G7 or G8	−0.0744*** (0.0249)	−0.0165 (0.0365)	−0.0480 (0.0380)
Observations	3,642	1,784	978

NOTE: Each model includes a set of cohort indicators. Standard errors, adjusted for clustering at the school level, are in parentheses. * = statistically significant at the 10-percent level. ** = statistically significant at the 5-percent level. *** = statistically significant at the 1-percent level.

Table 4.3
Probit Estimates of Attending a Two-Year or Four-Year College Within Five Years (coefficient estimates are marginal effects)

Variable	Florida	Chicago
Attend charter HS	0.0824*** (0.0289)	0.1028 (0.0509)
Math score, G8	0.0013*** (0.0005)	0.0017** (0.0010)
Reading score, G8	0.0024*** (0.0004)	0.0028*** (0.0008)
Female	0.0867*** (0.0299)	0.0696** (0.0317)
African American	0.0641* (0.0371)	0.1651* (0.0801)
Hispanic	0.1804*** (0.0533)	−0.0314 (0.1146)
Asian	0.2895** (0.1044)	
LEP/bilingual, G8	−0.2880** (0.0855)	0.1474* (0.0836)
Special ed, G8	0.0420 (0.0432)	−0.0290 (0.0660)
Free/reduced-price lunch, G8	−0.1577*** (0.0259)	−0.0130 (0.0716)
Changed schools, G7 or G8	−0.0471 (0.0314)	−0.0705 (0.0417)
Observations	1,787	695

NOTE: * = statistically significant at the 10-percent level. ** = statistically significant at the 5-percent level. *** = statistically significant at the 1-percent level.

the coefficients, we provide an example. If the analysis produces a positive coefficient estimate of 0.01 for students attending charter schools, the interpretation of this coefficient is that charter-school students are 1 percentage point more likely to graduate than noncharter students. If, alternatively, the analysis produces a −0.01 coefficient, the interpretation is just the opposite. For continuous variables, the coefficient represents the change in probability from a one-unit change in the independent variable. For instance, for test scores, the coefficient represents the change in probability from a one-unit change in the scaled test scores.

The estimated models include controls for student demographics, English language skills, special education–program participation, family income (i.e., free or reduced-price lunch status), and mobility during middle school. Student ability and prior educational inputs are accounted for by inclusion of eighth-grade test scores in math and reading.

The estimated impact of charter–high school attendance on the probability of obtaining a high-school diploma is positive in both Florida and Chicago. In Chicago, students who switched from a charter middle school to a charter high school were 7 percentage points more likely to earn a regular high-school diploma than their counterparts with similar observable characteristics who attended a traditional public high school. The graduation differential for Florida charter schools was even higher at 12 to 15 percentage points, depending on whether a four- or five-year window for graduation is used.

The findings for college attendance, presented in Table 4.3, are remarkably similar in Florida and Chicago. A student who attended a charter school in eighth grade and transitioned to a charter high school in ninth grade is 8 to 10 percentage points more likely to attend a postsecondary institution within five years of starting high school than a similar student who attended a traditional public high school.[6]

In the results presented thus far, possible selection bias is mitigated in two ways. First, by including student and family characteristics as explanatory variables, we control for observable differences between

[6] We also estimated the college-attendance model using a six-year window. Tracking students six years past eighth grade reduces the number of cohorts and thus attenuates the sample size significantly, particularly in Chicago. Using the six-year window, the effect of charter–high school attendance on college attendance remains positive and significant in the Florida sample but is positive and statistically insignificant in the Chicago sample. Using the six-year-window sample in Chicago but estimating the probability of attending college within five years of eighth grade yields similar results, suggesting that the differential effects between the five-year and six-year estimates are due to the reduction in sample size rather than to the increase in the length of the window in which to observe college attendance.

students who attend charter high schools and those who go to traditional public high schools. Second, by limiting the sample to students who attended a charter school in eighth grade, we indirectly control for time-invariant unobserved student or family traits that may be correlated with charter-school attendance. Put differently, if family preferences do not change significantly over time, then limiting the sample to charter–middle school attendees effectively controls for unobserved family traits at the high-school level. However, there still exists the possibility that observed changes occur between eighth and ninth grades that influence both high-school choice and subsequent educational attainment. For example, dissatisfaction with performance in a charter middle school that is not captured by test scores (e.g., discipline issues or a poor fit between the student's interests or ability and the curriculum being offered) could lead parents to choose to send their child to a traditional public high school and be correlated with later performance in high school. Depending on the forces behind high-school choice, this could impart either a negative or a positive bias on the estimated impact of charter–high school attendance on educational attainment. To consider this possibility and develop further safeguards against selection bias, we next explore the determinants of high-school choice.

Determinants of Charter–High School Attendance. As demonstrated by Neal (1997), Grogger and Neal (2000) and Altonji, Elder, and Taber (2005), high-school choice is determined in part by physical proximity. In the charter context, this can play out in two ways. First, some charter schools offer both middle- and high-school grades, effectively making the transition cost zero.[7] Second, when a student must switch schools to attend high school, distance can vary greatly; the nearest charter high school may be down the street or many miles away.

In examining the transition patterns of students based on the range of grades that were offered by the charter school they attended in

---

[7] While most charter schools offering middle- and high-school classes have all grades in the same location, this is not universal. In a few instances, there can be one common administration but the high-school campus may be physically separate from the middle-school campus.

grade 8, we observe, as expected, students whose eighth-grade school also offered at least some high-school grades were much more likely to attend a charter school in grade 9 than were students who had to switch schools in order to continue in a charter in grade 9. In Florida, about 57 percent of students whose charter school offered some or all high-school grades went to a charter high school, whereas only 20 percent of students whose charter middle school did not offer high-school grades continued on to a charter high school. In Chicago, eighth-grade charter-school students were generally more likely to attend a charter high school, but the relative transition rates based on grade availability are similar to those in Florida. In Chicago, 74 percent of students whose eighth-grade charter offered grade 9 attended a charter school in grade 9, whereas the proportion of students who had to go to a different school in grade 9 and chose to attend a charter school was only 25 percent. Clearly, the ability to remain in the same school has a large impact on high-school choice.

We can also measure the physical proximity of other charter high schools and thereby gauge the effect of distance on high-school choice. Further, for Florida, we can determine the proximity of traditional public high schools. Table 4.4 provides information on the number of TPS and charter-school options available to Florida students within 10, 5, and 2.5 miles of the charter school they attended in grade 8. As expected, students who go on to a charter school in grade 9 have fewer TPS options and more charter schools from which to choose within a given distance than do students who transition to TPSs.

In Table 4.5, we present probit estimates of the choice of attending a charter school in grade 9 as a function of both the grade offerings of a student's middle school and the availability of other school alternatives. Consistent with the summary statistics presented in Table 4.4, the availability of ninth grade in the same school a student attended in eighth grade has the largest impact on the likelihood of attending a charter school in grade 9, raising the probability from 18 to 46 percentage points, depending on the jurisdiction and the size of the geographic area under consideration. The number of other charter schools offering grade 9 always carries a positive coefficient, though the effect is

Table 4.4
Mean Number of Schools Offering Grade 9, by Student Transition Type (based on location of charter school student attended in grade 8 and location of schools offering grade 9 in year after eighth-grade attendance)

	Florida			
	Transition to Traditional		Transition to Charter	
Variable	Obs.	Mean	Obs.	Mean
Number of TPSs within 10 miles offering G9	2,912	22.29	1,304	20.87
Charter that student attended in G8 offers G9 within 10 miles	2,912	0.51	1,304	0.84
Number of other charter schools within 10 miles offering G9	2,912	2.11	1,304	3.34
Number of TPSs within 5 miles offering G9	2,912	8.56	1,304	6.09
Charter that student attended in G8 offers G9 within 5 miles	2,912	0.50	1,304	0.80
Number of other charter schools within 5 miles offering G9	2,912	1.12	1,304	2.19
Number of TPSs within 2.5 miles offering G9	2,912	3.47	1,304	1.76
Charter that student attended in G8 offers G9 within 2.5 miles	2,912	0.50	1,304	0.80
Number of other charter schools within 2.5 miles offering G9	2,912	0.60	1,304	1.04

significant only for the five-mile radius in Chicago.[8] Within Florida, the availability of a traditional public high school within either 2.5 miles or 5 miles of the student's middle school has a significant negative correlation with charter–high school attendance, as one would expect if the two are substitutes. Holding constant the number of charter schools within a given area, distance to the nearest charter high

[8] The fact that high-school choice is not significantly affected by having additional charter–high school options nearby suggests that the diversity among charter high schools may be less than the difference between charters and traditional public high schools.

Table 4.5
Probit Estimates of Attending a Charter High School in Grade 9, Based on Minimum Distance and Number of Schools of Given Type in Surrounding Area Offering Grade 9 in Relevant Year (coefficient estimates are marginal effects)

	Florida			Chicago	
Variable	10 mi.	5 mi.	2.5 mi.	5 mi.	2.5 mi.
Distance to nearest TPS	0.0374 (0.0386)	0.0192 (0.0260)	−0.0026 (0.0230)		
Distance to nearest other charter	−0.0048 (0.0032)	−0.0043* (0.0025)	−0.0041* (0.0023)	0.0371 (0.0441)	0.0378 (0.0655)
Number of TPSs	−0.0057 (0.0037)	−0.0198** (0.0097)	−0.0680*** (0.0266)		
Number of other charters	0.0252 (0.0276)	0.0418 (0.0373)	0.0154 (0.0517)	0.1161* (0.0704)	0.2825 (0.3565)
G8 charter offers G9	0.2462*** (0.0820)	0.1833** (0.0810)	0.1763** (0.0897)	0.4616*** (0.1093)	0.4110* (0.1988)
Observations	4,216	4,216	4,216	978	978
Pseudo R-squared	0.18	0.20	0.22	0.22	0.22

NOTE: Standard errors, adjusted for clustering at the school level, are in parentheses. * = statistically significant at the 10-percent level. ** = statistically significant at the 5-percent level. *** = statistically significant at the 1-percent level.

school appears to affect school choice as well.[9] For both the 2.5-mile and 5-mile radii, distance to other charter schools offering grade 9 is negatively correlated with charter attendance in ninth grade in Florida, as one would expect. For example, using the five-mile radius, having a charter high school one mile away from a student's middle school rather than five miles away would increase the probability of attending a charter school in ninth grade by 1.6 percentage points. Perhaps due to

[9] In Florida, if the distance to the nearest school of a given type exceeded 25 miles, the minimum-distance measure was assigned a value of 99.

the urban setting, distance to other charter schools is not a significant factor in Chicago.

Bivariate Probit Estimates of the Determinants of Educational Attainment. Bivariate probit regressions of educational attainment are presented in Tables 4.6 and 4.7.[10] For the charter–high school attendance equation, we use the 2.5-mile radius specification from Table 4.5 for both Florida and Chicago, since it provided the best fit. However, we obtain very similar results if we instead use the five-mile-radius specification. The attainment equations are the same as those estimated by single-equation probit analysis in Tables 4.2 and 4.3. We continue to find significant positive correlations between charter–high school attendance and both receipt of a high-school diploma and college attendance (although, in Florida, the effect of college attendance is significant only at the 10-percent level). The magnitude of the effects are quite large, roughly double the size of the estimates from the single-equation probit.

The larger estimated coefficients in the bivariate probit model as well as the negative estimated cross-equation correlations (rho) indicate a negative selection bias in both Florida and Chicago. To the extent that there is self-selection, it is the students who are less likely to graduate (conditional on observed characteristics) who are choosing to attend charter high schools.[11] This is somewhat counterintuitive, particularly in Florida, where the descriptive statistics presented in Table 4.1 suggest a positive selection bias with respect to important observable student characteristics. Florida charter–middle school students who go on to charter high schools tend to have higher eighth-grade test scores and are less likely to be receiving free or reduced-price lunches

---

[10] The bivariate probit allows the unobserved determinants of high-school choice and educational attainment to be correlated by assuming that the errors from the high school–choice and high school–graduation or college-attendance models are distributed bivariate normal. See Evans and Schwab (1995).

[11] Interestingly, Neal (1997), as do other papers in the Catholic–high school literature he cites, also finds a negative selection effect. Neal conjectures that affluent parents with strong preferences for educational quality are more likely to live in suburban areas with elite public schools and thus Catholic high schools may not attract students with the best (unobserved) traits.

Table 4.6
Bivariate Probit Estimates of Receiving a Standard High-School Diploma (coefficient estimates are marginal effects)

	Florida		Chicago
Variable	**Within 4 Years**	**Within 5 Years**	**Within 5+ Years**
Attend charter HS	0.31*** (0.05)	0.33*** (0.06)	0.15*** (0.05)
Math score, G8	0.003*** (0.0003)	0.003*** (0.0005)	0.0008** (0.0004)
Reading score, G8	0.002*** (0.0003)	0.002*** (0.0003)	0.001*** (0.0003)
Female	0.07*** (0.02)	0.04* (0.02)	0.03** (0.02)
African American	0.08*** (0.02)	0.13*** (0.04)	0.09** (0.04)
Hispanic	0.08*** (0.03)	0.12*** (0.05)	0.03 (0.05)
Asian	0.09 (0.09)	0.08 (0.14)	
LEP, G8	0.07 (0.09)	0.12 (0.14)	0.02 (0.04)
Special ed, G8	0.08** (0.03)	0.07* (0.04)	0.04** (0.02)
Free/reduced-price lunch, G8	−0.15*** (0.02)	−0.11*** (0.03)	−0.01 (0.03)
Changed schools, G7 or G8	−0.06*** (0.02)	−0.004 (0.03)	−0.02 (0.02)
Rho	−0.46*** (0.12)	−0.53*** (0.13)	−0.49*** (0.19)
Observations	3,640	1,783	978

NOTE: Each model includes a set of cohort indicators. Standard errors, which equal the marginal effects divided by the bivariate probit z-scores (adjusted for clustering at the school level), are in parentheses. The equation for the 2.5-mile radius reported in Table 4.5 is used to predict charter–high school attendance. * = statistically significant at the 10-percent level. ** = statistically significant at the 5-percent level. *** = statistically significant at the 1-percent level.

Table 4.7
Bivariate Probit Estimates of Attending a Two-Year or Four-Year College Within Five Years (coefficient estimates are marginal effects)

Variable	Florida	Chicago
Attend charter HS	0.18* (0.11)	0.14*** (0.04)
Math score, G8	0.001*** (0.0005)	0.0006 (0.0005)
Reading score, G8	0.002*** (0.0004)	0.0011** (0.0005)
Female	0.09*** (0.03)	0.03* (0.02)
African American	0.08* (0.04)	0.08** (0.03)
Hispanic	0.19*** (0.05)	−0.002 (0.05)
Asian	0.27** (0.13)	
LEP/bilingual, G8	−0.29** (0.12)	0.08* (0.05)
Special ed, G8	0.04 (0.04)	−0.02 (0.03)
Free/reduced-price lunch, G8	−0.15*** (0.03)	−0.01 (0.03)
Changed schools, G7 or G8	−0.04 (0.03)	−0.02 (0.02)
Rho	−0.21 (0.19)	−0.49* (0.25)
Observations	1,786	695

NOTE: Each model includes a set of cohort indicators. Standard errors, which equal the marginal effects divided by the bivariate probit z-scores (adjusted for clustering at the school level), are in parentheses. The equation for the 2.5-mile radius reported in Table 4.5 is used to predict charter–high school attendance. * = statistically significant at the 10-percent level. ** = statistically significant at the 5-percent level. *** = statistically significant at the 1-percent level.

(a proxy for poverty) than those students who transition to traditional public high schools.[12] We can only speculate as to why this is so. It is possible that parents whose children have demonstrated academic ability in middle school but whose unobserved personal traits pose a risk of dropping out are more likely to choose charter high schools in a belief that the TPS environment would make it more likely that their child leaves school early. As one example, suppose that some children earn high marks in middle school but are relatively immature and might be easily swayed by negative peer influences in high school. Parents of these children might opt for a charter high school in the belief that it will provide an environment with better peers.

Even if one doubts the relatively large estimated magnitudes of the impact of charter high schools on graduation and college attendance from the bivariate probit models, the results from the various models presented all point toward a substantial positive effect of charter–high school attendance on educational attainment.

Robustness Checks. As just described, graduation indicators (and college attendance in Chicago) were imputed for students whose graduation status could not be directly determined because they left the public schools or moved out of the jurisdiction. This was done to avoid potential attrition bias. We show in Tables 4.8 (Florida) and 4.9 (Chicago), however, that simply dropping students whose educational attainment is unknown and not imputing any values yields qualitatively similar results.

Given that charter high schools tend to be much smaller than traditional public high schools, school size and charter status may be confounded in our baseline analysis. Put differently, what appear to be charter-school effects could simply be school-size effects. In order to disentangle the effects of school size and school type on educational attainment, we re-estimated the high school–graduation and

---

[12] Comparisons on other observable characteristics in Florida are mixed. For example, the fraction of blacks is higher among those attending traditional public high schools, whereas the proportions of Hispanics and of LEP students are higher for the group attending charter high schools. In Chicago, there is a tendency toward negative sorting on observables, with students who attend charter high schools having somewhat lower eighth-grade test scores than those students who go on to traditional public high schools.

Table 4.8
Probit and Bivariate Probit Estimates of the Relationship Between Charter–High School Attendance and Educational Attainment in Florida from Alternative Samples and Models (coefficient estimates are marginal effects)

	HS Diploma Within 4 Years		Attend College Within 5 Years	
Model	**Probit**	**Bivariate Probit**	**Probit**	**Bivariate Probit**
Baseline (full sample), attend charter HS	0.12*** (0.03)	0.31*** (0.05)	0.08** (0.03)	0.18* (0.11)
Baseline (without imputing missing values), attend charter HS	0.15*** (0.04)	0.33*** (0.06)	0.08*** (0.03)	0.18* (0.11)
With controls for school size (full sample), attend charter HS	0.17*** (0.03)	0.33*** (0.05)	0.11*** (0.03)	0.18* (0.10)
With controls for G10 test score (full sample), attend charter HS	0.05* (0.02)	0.12*** (0.04)	0.09** (0.04)	0.14* (0.08)
Baseline (only students whose G8 charter does not offer G9), attend charter HS	0.13*** (0.04)	0.22*** (0.07)	0.11** (0.04)	0.30*** (0.11)
Allowing differential effect of conversion charter high schools (full sample)				
Attend charter HS	0.08** (0.03)	0.28*** (0.06)	0.09** (0.04)	0.20** (0.10)
Attend conversion charter HS	0.15*** (0.03)	0.08*** (0.03)	−0.02 (0.04)	−0.05 (0.06)

NOTE: Each model includes the explanatory variables delineated in Table 4.3 and a set of cohort indicators. Standard errors, adjusted for clustering at the school level, are in parentheses. * = statistically significant at the 10-percent level. ** = statistically significant at the 5-percent level. *** = statistically significant at the 1-percent level.

college-attendance models with an additional control for the total number of students attending the school. The results, presented in Tables 4.8 and 4.9, are comparable to those from the baseline model, indicating that the estimated charter–high school differentials are not due to differences in school size.

Table 4.9
Probit and Bivariate Probit Estimates of the Relationship Between Charter–High School Attendance and Educational Attainment in Chicago from Alternative Samples and Models (coefficient estimates are marginal effects)

	HS Diploma Within 4 Years		Attend College Within 5 Years	
Model	Probit	Bivariate Probit	Probit	Bivariate Probit
Baseline (full sample), attend charter HS	0.07** (0.03)	0.15*** (0.05)	0.10** (0.05)	0.14*** (0.04)
Baseline (without imputing missing values), attend charter HS	0.11*** (0.04)	0.15*** (0.06)	0.13** (0.06)	0.15*** (0.05)
With controls for school size (full sample), attend charter HS	0.06* (0.03)	0.14*** (0.05)	0.07* (0.04)	0.13*** (0.03)
With controls for G10 test score (full sample), attend charter HS	0.06* (0.03)	0.14*** (0.05)	0.09* (0.05)	0.13*** (0.04)

NOTE: Each model includes the explanatory variables delineated in Table 4.3 and a set of cohort indicators. Standard errors, adjusted for clustering at the school level, are in parentheses. * = statistically significant at the 10-percent level. ** = statistically significant at the 5-percent level. *** = statistically significant at the 1-percent level.

We attempt to distinguish between pure achievement effects and educational-attainment effects of charters by including controls for 10th-grade math and reading achievement scores. As indicated by the estimates reported in the fourth panel of Tables 4.8 and 4.9, controlling for 10th-grade test scores explains about half the charter–high school graduation differential in Florida but less than 20 percent of the difference in Chicago. Controlling for 10th-grade test scores has an even smaller effect on the estimated impact of charter–high school attendance on college enrollment, altering the estimated magnitude by only about 10 percent each in Florida and Chicago. This suggests that the differential effects of charter schools on educational attainment are not due solely to measured achievement differences in charter and traditional public high schools.[13]

In the TPS sector in both Chicago and Florida, high schools are almost always separate from middle schools. This is not the case for charter schools, as noted previously. As a result, as reported in Table 4.4, about 30 percent of Florida charter eighth-grade students attended schools that also offered at least some high-school grades. In Chicago, nearly half of the eighth-grade charter-school students could attend at least some high-school grades (grades 9–12) without changing schools. Indeed, more than 70 percent of the Chicago students who attended charter schools in both grades 8 and 9 were in schools offering both middle-school and high-school grades. This raises the concern that the measured effects of charter–high school attendance on educational attainment could simply reflect advantages of grouping middle- and high-school grades together rather than differences in curriculum, organization, or employment practices between charters and TPSs.

To disentangle grade-configuration effects from pure charter-school effects, we restricted the Florida sample to those students whose eighth-grade charter school did not offer grade 9 and re-estimated both the simple probit and bivariate probit models of high-school graduation and college attendance.[14] The resulting estimates are presented in the fifth panel of Table 4.8. For high-school graduation, restricting the sample produces estimates of the univariate probit model that are nearly identical to the original estimates. In the bivariate probit model using the restricted sample, the estimates are about 30-percent smaller than when using the full sample. In both the univariate and bivariate models of high-school graduation, the restricted-sample estimates of charter–high school attendance are statistically significant at very high confidence levels. In contrast, estimates of the effect of charter–high school attendance on college enrollment are higher in the restricted sample compared to the original sample that includes schools offer-

[13] We also separately estimated the relationship between charter–high school attendance and student achievement. Results are reported in Tables C.4 and C.5 in Appendix C.

[14] Since schools offering grade 9 are removed from the sample, the first stage of the bivariate probit excludes the "eighth-grade charter offers G9" variable.

ing both eighth and ninth grades. As with the high school–graduation estimates, the estimated coefficients on the charter–high school variables in the college-enrollment models remain statistically significant at better than 95-percent confidence levels. These findings suggest that, while combining middle- and high-school grades may enhance the likelihood of high-school graduation (at least in the charter sector), the positive association between charter–high school attendance and educational attainment is not due primarily to differences in grade configurations between charters and TPSs.

Another potential concern is that a number of charter schools in Florida are former TPSs that converted to charter status. If conversion schools were better-than-average TPSs to begin with, they may be distorting the estimated impact of charters on educational attainment. In order to allow for a differential impact of conversion charters, we added a conversion charter interaction term and re-estimated the graduation and college-attendance equations. As indicated in the last panel of Table 4.8, conversion charters have significantly greater effects on high-school graduation than do de novo charters, though the impact of nonconversion charters is still sizable in magnitude (nearly equal to the estimate in Chicago) and significant at better than a 95-percent confidence level. For college attendance, we observe no significant differential impact of attending a conversion charter, and the correlation between attending a de novo charter and college attendance is still positive and significant at better than a 95-percent confidence level.

Chapter Summary

In this chapter, we found that charter–high school attendance is associated with a higher probability of successful high-school completion and an increased likelihood of attending a two- or four-year college in two disparate jurisdictions, Florida and Chicago. These results are based exclusively on the examination of students who were enrolled in charter schools prior to high school, so there is uncertainty about their generalizability to charter–high school students who were previously enrolled in conventional middle schools. Nonetheless, the results suggest that charter high schools in these two locations are producing substantial attainment benefits for many of their students. The reasons for these effects are not clear. We show that they are not driven by the smaller size of charter schools and are only partially explained by achievement differences between charters and TPSs. These results—and their similarity to results in the Catholic-school literature—suggest the possible value of seeking to replicate characteristics that charter and Catholic high schools have in common, which include not only small size but also (perhaps) a clear sense of educational mission—i.e., the kinds of features that have long been identified as characteristic of effective high schools (see, e.g., P. Hill, Foster, and Gendler, 1990; Bryk, Lee, and Holland, 1993).

CHAPTER FIVE

Competitive Effects of Charter Schools on Student Achievement in Traditional Public Schools

Supporters of charter schools often argue that they create healthy competition in the K–12 education market, creating incentives for TPSs to improve their performance. Detractors doubt that competition induces positive results and worry that, instead, the siphoning of resources to charter schools will undermine the performance of TPSs and thereby harm their students. The empirical evidence on this key issue of contention is minimal, with only a few studies that attempt to gauge the systemic effect of charter schools.

The studies that have examined systemic effects have used school-level measures of competition, such as the distance from the charter school to nearby public schools or the proportion of the district's students who are enrolled in charter schools. Hoxby (2002) and Bettinger (2005) used school-level outcomes to estimate competitive effects, while Holmes, DeSimone, and Rupp (2003); Bifulco and Ladd (2006); Sass (2006); and Booker, Gilpatric, et al. (2005) used student-level data for more-refined analyses of competition in North Carolina, Florida, and Texas. Generally, these studies found small, positive competitive effects or no effects on students in nearby TPSs.

Another RAND study also examined competitive effects in California using survey responses from TPSs that assessed whether the school felt any competitive pressures from charter schools and, if so, what changes the school had made in response (Buddin and Zimmer, forthcoming). It also used student-level data and proximity of charter schools to TPSs. Through both approaches, the study authors found no evidence of competitive effects in California.

While these analyses have provided a better understanding of competition, these studies have focused on only one state at a time, and competitive effects may vary across states and laws, for two reasons. First, there is considerable variation across the country in the extent to which school-district enrollments are growing or shrinking. In rapidly growing districts with capacity challenges, charter schools may act more like a release valve than a source of competitive pressure. These districts may welcome the introduction of charter schools as way of dealing with overcrowding. Districts facing stable or declining enrollments, in contrast, may seek to keep all of their students. In these cases, charter schools may exert real pressure on public schools.

Second, the specific details of charter laws and policies may determine the extent to which school districts feel competitive pressure. For instance, some states have hold-harmless laws, in which districts do not lose the associated money when the student transfers to a charter school, providing little financial incentive for the TPSs to compete for students. Charter laws may be more or less restrictive in the freedoms that they grant charter schools, which may affect their ability to innovate and compete. And some states have caps on the number of charter schools, which may restrict the ability for charter schools to exert competitive effects.

Analytical Details

Studies examining competitive effects typically assume that competitive effects will be felt most strongly in TPSs that are in close proximity to charter schools (Bifulco and Ladd, 2006; Sass, 2006; Buddin and Zimmer, forthcoming; Holmes, DeSimone, and Rupp, 2003; Booker, Gilpatric, et al., 2005). Building on this research, we use two proxies for competitive pressure. First, we use a measure of the distance to the nearest charter school. Presumably, the closer a TPS is to a charter school, the more likely it is that the school will feel competitive pressure. Second, we examine whether the level of charter-school presence within a local educational market affects student achievement within

TPSs by examining the number of charter schools within 2.5 miles of a TPS.

Any analysis of competitive effects is complicated by the fact that charter schools may not randomly locate, but rather locate near low-performing TPSs. Analyzing the effects of charter proxies without controlling for the unobserved TPS characteristics that have led these schools to be low performing may bias downward the estimate of the effect that charter schools are having on students in TPSs. In addition, it is important to control for both observed and unobserved student characteristics associated with student performance. To achieve both of these objectives, we include both student and school fixed effects, thereby controlling for time-invariant characteristics of students, such as race or ethnicity and family motivation, as well as time-invariant school characteristics, such as the environment of the neighborhood and quality of the facilities. To incorporate both student and school fixed effects, we run a model with a combined student and school fixed effect known as a spell effect, which represents each unique student/school combination. Each student's time of enrollment in a particular school is viewed as a spell. Competitive effects are, therefore, estimated by examining the growth of achievement of the same students in the same schools as the level of charter competition varies over time.[1]

The competitive analysis is specified in Equation 5.1:

$$A_{jt} - A_{jt-1} = \alpha Comp_{jt} + \mu_j + \theta_{gt} + \nu_{jt}, \qquad (5.1)$$

where $A_{jt} - A_{jt-1}$ is a measure of the achievement gains of the *j*th student in the *t*th year, $Comp_{jt}$ is one of the two measures of charter competition (each run in a separate model) of the *j*th student in the *t*th year, μ_j captures unique student/school fixed effects, θ_{gt} captures grade-by-year fixed effects, and ν is the random disturbance term.[2]

1 The spell effects should also control for other sources of competition within the district, such as private schools and magnet schools, to the extent that these sources of competition remain constant over time.

2 Because individual student observations within schools may not be independent, we run the analysis by clustering students by schools to create robust standard errors.

In the model, the competitive effect of charter schools on TPS students is identified by observing changes in the achievement trajectories of individual students when their TPSs experience changes in the number of charter schools within a concentric distance or the proximity of the nearest charter school.

It is conceivable that charter schools could produce competitive effects in TPSs that are not captured by our methods. Our approach assumes that charter schools produce competitive pressure through their proximity to TPSs. But competitive effects may manifest themselves through the introduction of charter schools anywhere within a district, if the actors most likely to feel competitive effects are district officials rather than principals or teachers (which might occur because the resource shift associated with charter schools occurs at the district level); we lack comprehensive data on school-district boundaries that might permit examination of a district-based measure of competition. Moreover, competitive effects may manifest with the mere threat of charter schools appearing on the landscape, rather than the actual opening of charter schools; our method cannot capture such a threat effect. Furthermore, in areas with growing enrollment, charter schools could act as a release valve for overcrowding schools. In these cases, we would not expect much competitive pressure. Finally, our analysis also assumes that competitive effects appear immediately with no lag. It could take time before any effects appear. Because of these uncertainties, we regard the results in this chapter as suggestive but not definitive.

The results of the analysis are displayed in Table 5.1. The interpretation of the coefficients varies by the charter proxy. For distance to nearest charter school, the coefficient is the achievement gain of TPS students, measured in changes in the standardized z-score, for each mile away from a charter school. For the number of charter schools, the interpretation is the gains in z-scores for each additional charter school within 2.5 miles of the TPS the student attends.

Across the geographic locations, only Texas shows evidence that charter schools are creating any competitive effects for TPSs, and, even in Texas, the estimated effects are small. This suggests, first of

Table 5.1
Estimates of Competitive Effects

Variable	Math Coefficient (robust standard error)	Reading Coefficient (robust standard error)
Chicago		
Distance to nearest charter school	0.00 (0.01)	−0.01 (0.01)
Number of charter schools within 2.5 miles	0.01 (0.02)	0.02 (0.01)
Denver		
Distance to nearest charter school	0.00 (0.04)	0.01 (0.03)
Number of charter schools within 2.5 miles	0.03 (0.02)	0.01 (0.01)
Milwaukee		
Distance to nearest charter school	−0.02 (0.02)	0.01 (0.02)
Number of charter schools within 2.5 miles	0.00 (0.01)	0.00 (0.01)
Philadelphia		
Distance to nearest charter school	0.01 (0.06)	0.06 (0.05)
Number of charter schools within 2.5 miles	0.01 (0.02)	0.00 (0.01)
San Diego		
Distance to nearest charter school	0.00 (0.01)	0.01 (0.005)
Number of charter schools within 2.5 miles	−0.01 (0.01)	0.00 (0.01)
Ohio		
Distance to nearest charter school	0.00 (0.005)	0.00 (0.003)
Number of charter schools within 2.5 miles	−0.02 (0.02)	0.02 (0.01)

Table 5.1—Continued

Variable	Math Coefficient (robust standard error)	Reading Coefficient (robust standard error)
Texas		
Distance to nearest charter school	−0.0002 (0.0002)	0.0004 (0.0003)
Number of charter schools within 2.5 miles	0.03** (0.003)	0.02** (0.003)

NOTE: ** = statistically significant at the 5-percent level.

all, that our estimates of the direct achievement impacts of charter schools, reported in Chapter Four, are generally not biased downward by competitive effects that are raising scores in comparison TPSs. More importantly, it also means that, although we find little evidence of a positive impact of competition, neither do we find any evidence of the negative impact hypothesized by some of the opponents of charter schools. Across all of the jurisdictions examined, despite variation in funding mechanisms and the extent of funding transfers from TPSs to charter schools, we find no evidence that students who remain in TPSs experience an achievement decline as a result of the growth of charter schools nearby.

CHAPTER SIX

Implications for Policy and Research

Charter schools continue to be hotly debated, but rigorous research on charter-school impacts has only recently begun to inform the debate. The number of well-designed impact studies is growing, but the accumulated knowledge base remains thin. Long-term attainment outcomes have not been examined; the sorting of students by race and ability has been infrequently studied; the possible (positive or negative) systemic effect of charter schools on students who remain in TPSs has received little empirical attention; and the relationships between the details of state charter policies and the impacts produced have not been identified. Finally and most importantly, questions about the validity of the findings of even the best-designed charter-school impact studies have remained, producing deep uncertainty about the interpretation of results. Findings of different studies have differed, but it is not clear whether the conflicting conclusions reflect genuinely different effects of charter schools in different geographic locations with varying charter laws and policies or, instead, reflect varying research approaches—some of which may be methodologically biased.

We set out to address some of these gaps in the existing research by examining four primary research questions across a number of geographic locations: (1) What are the characteristics of students transferring to charter schools? (2) What effect do charter schools have on test-score gains for students who transfer between TPSs and charter schools? (3) What is the effect of attending a charter high school on the probability of graduating and of entering college? (4) What effect does the introduction of charter schools have on test scores of students in nearby TPSs? Finally, in this chapter, we discuss similarities and differences in charter-school effects across locations, considering whether any observed differences in effects might be related to differences in local charter laws and policies. In conducting these analyses, we also shed light on key research and methodological issues relevant to past and future studies that aim to estimate the achievement effects of charter schools.

We begin this chapter by summarizing the key findings related to the various research questions, and then turn to policy and methodological implications.

Key Findings

We find no evidence that charter schools are systematically attracting above-average students. The prior test scores of students transferring into charter schools were near or below local (districtwide or statewide) averages in every geographic location included in the study. In terms of prior achievement, in most sites, the transferring students did not differ substantially from other students in the TPSs they left: In a few sites, they were slightly higher achieving than their former peers; in other sites, they were slightly lower achieving; and, in Ohio and Texas, they were much lower achieving than their former peers. White students, who constituted a minority of charter entrants in all sites, deviated from the general pattern somewhat: In most sites, white students entering charter schools were, on average, slightly higher achieving than the white students in their previous schools.

Transfers to charter schools do not involve dramatic shifts in the sorting of students by race in any of the sites included in the study. In most sites, the racial composition of the charter schools is similar to that of the TPSs from which the charter students are transferring. There is some variation: Transfers to charter schools tend to marginally reduce racial integration in Philadelphia while marginally increasing racial integration in Chicago. African American students transferring to charter schools move to schools with a higher concentration of African American students in five of seven locales. Across the seven locales, the (unweighted) average increase in the proportion of African American students experienced by African Americans who transfer to charter schools is 4 percentage points. The finding that African Americans tend to increase their racial isolation when moving to charter schools is consistent with previous findings in North Carolina (Bifulco and Ladd, 2007).

The average achievement effects of elementary charters are very difficult to assess in the absence of prekindergarten baseline test scores. For charter schools with entry grades at the middle- and high-school levels, we have greater confidence in the impact estimates. In five out of seven locales, nonprimary charter schools are producing achievement gains on par with those of local TPSs, though middle schools in Chicago and Texas appear to be falling short. We find no evidence that charter schools systematically produce different effects for different demographic groups.

Virtual charter schools, which use technology to deliver education to students in their homes and enroll a substantial portion of charter students in Ohio (and in Pennsylvania and California), merit additional attention. In Ohio, students have substantially lower achievement gains while attending virtual schools than they experienced in TPSs. However, this result should be interpreted cautiously because it might be biased by the unusual sample of students who enroll in virtual charter schools.

In most locations, charter schools have difficulty raising student achievement in their first year of operation, typically producing achievement results that fall short of those of local TPSs. This is consistent with prior research and common sense and may not be a charter-specific phenomenon: Opening a new school is challenging, regardless of whether the school is a charter school. Across the locations, the performance of charter schools as measured by their achievement generally improves after the first year of operation. In many instances, the improvement with experience is sufficient only to make the results less negative in the first year or to achieve parity with, rather than exceed, TPS performance.

Charter schools in most locales have marginally greater variation in performance than TPSs, as measured by the achievement-impact estimate for each school, and, in some locations, this may simply reflect greater mea-

surement error associated with the smaller average size of charter schools. Ohio is a notable exception: Its charter schools have a much wider range of variation in performance than its TPSs.

In the two locations with data on educational attainment outcomes (Florida and Chicago), attending a charter high school is associated with statistically significant and substantial increases in the probability of graduating and of enrolling in college. Among students who attended a charter middle school (who are the only ones for whom we can convincingly estimate an impact), those who went on to attend a charter high school were 7 to 15 percentage points more likely to graduate than students who transitioned to a traditional public high school (controlling for observed student characteristics and test scores). Similarly, those attending a charter high school were 8 to 10 percentage points more likely to enroll in college. We cannot be certain that these positive effects are also experienced by charter–high school students who attend traditional middle schools. Nevertheless, our positive results are promising and are not fully explained by estimated impacts on test scores, suggesting that researchers and policymakers need to look beyond test scores to fully assess charter schools' performance. In one of the two locations (Chicago), the estimated positive attainment effects could be related (at least in part) to eliminating the school transition between middle school and high school.

There is no evidence in any of the locations that charter schools are negatively affecting the achievement of students in nearby TPSs. There is also little evidence of a positive competitive impact on nearby TPSs. Only in one location do we find any evidence of a statistically significant effect on TPSs of competitive pressure exerted by charter schools: In Texas, the estimate of competitive effects in one of two specifications is positive but small.

Policy Implications

With only eight sites included in the study, quantitative analysis of the relationships between state policy variables and measured outcomes is precluded. Nonetheless, the study can inform policy by identifying outcomes that are consistent across sites and by examining outliers in the context of possible policy influences. We emphasize the modifier *possible* in discussing policy influences: Strong causal inferences are difficult enough even in the analyses in Chapters Three and Four that aim to use the best available nonexperimental methods for calculating black-box estimates of charter-school effects in each site. Attempting to relate those estimates in a small number of states whose charter policies vary on a large number of dimensions is fraught with peril and necessarily speculative.

Findings (from Chapter Two) on the characteristics of students transferring to charter schools and the effects of those transfers on the mix of students in schools are largely consistent across the seven sites examined. In most locations, neither cream-skimming nor self-segregation need be feared. In all seven sites, students transferring to charter schools tended to choose schools with demographic characteristics not dramatically different from those of the TPSs they left. Similarly, differences in state charter policies did not lead to substantial differences in the kinds of students transferring to charter schools: They were relatively low-achieving students across the board. Relative to local averages, prior achievement levels of charter entrants were particularly low in Ohio and Texas. In the case of Texas, this could be attributable (at least in part) to the success of the provision in the state's original charter law encouraging the establishment of charter schools for disadvantaged students.

The estimates of the achievement impacts of nonprimary charter schools do not show great variation across sites. In most of the locales, average performance of charter schools is approximately on par with that of TPSs, providing little purchase on the policy levers that might serve to improve the performance of charter schools.

The only site in which charter schools deviate significantly, in both reading and math, from the average performance of TPSs, is Texas, where students who enter charter schools appear to be falling behind their own trajectories in TPSs. Among the seven states included in the achievement analyses, Texas has been scored highest on a measure of the flexibility of its charter law (Shober, Manna, and Witte, 2006). One might speculate that greater flexibility permitted the creation of a larger number of low-performing charter schools. But Texas also scored highest among the seven states on an index of the extent of local oversight of charter schools (data provided in private correspondence with Arnold Shober), and an alternative speculation might suggest that local oversight shackled charter schools that might otherwise be more effective. A third possible explanation is that the Texas Education Agency, which authorizes many charter schools, has been hampered by very limited resources (Mead and Rotherham, 2007). In the absence of impact estimates from many more states, these hypotheses must remain speculative.

Although the average impacts of charter schools provide little evidence on promising policy levers, some of the complementary achievement-impact analyses in Chapter Three suggest useful guidance for policymakers. Patterns in the achievement of charter schools by age suggest that experience matters: New charter schools generally perform poorly and improve after the first year of operation. The pattern of these results across states provides considerable grist for policy discussions. Policymakers in every state with a charter law should be looking for ways to dampen the negative achievement impacts that are so frequently experienced by students enrolled in first-year charters.

Although we do not have empirical evidence to point to specific methods that have been shown to smooth the challenges of the first year of a charter school's operation, it is not hard to imagine possibilities. For example, states might create or reinforce systems to disseminate information about key factors in charter start-up. Or they might require charter authorizers to create tighter screening of proposed charters to ensure that the school has a strong plan for the start-up period. Or they might increase funding for grants that newly awarded charter operators can use to pay start-up costs. Or they might encourage charters to open one grade per year, to reduce the scope of the first-year challenge. Or, finally, they might reduce the sector's reliance on brand-new schools and bring in experienced operators by making it easier for existing public and private schools to become charter schools.

The achievement-impact results also suggest that policymakers in states that permit virtual charter schools should closely examine their performance. Virtual charter schools represent the kind of instructional innovation that many advocates of charter schools hoped to promote, but our estimates in Ohio of their achievement impacts give cause for concern about whether their innovations are educationally effective. The consistency of the negative impacts of virtual schools in Ohio with the findings of a previous RAND study in California (Zimmer, Buddin, et al., 2003) buttresses these concerns.

The wide range of the performance of individual charter schools in Ohio likewise suggests policy implications. Greater variation in charter-school performance in Ohio is not entirely explained by its virtual charter schools. It may be related to the fact that the state's charter law allows an unusually diverse group of organizations to serve as charter authorizers (Russo, 2005); the performance of the authorizers probably varies substantially. It is also possible that the high variation in performance of Ohio's charters is partly related to resource constraints: A Thomas B. Fordham Institute report (2005) found that Ohio's funding scheme for charter schools leaves them at a "severe" disadvantage relative to TPSs.

In one sense, the variance in performance creates a policy opportunity in Ohio and any other state that experiences a similarly wide range of charter-school performance: Eliminating the lowest-performing charter schools has the potential to improve average results in such states substantially. This may not be easy; the challenge is to minimize the number of charter failures without sacrificing successful charter schools. Again, the empirical record does not identify any surefire solutions, but various possibilities could be tried. One set of policy levers might focus on improving the performance of charter authorizers, both at the stage of authorization and in subsequent reviews of school performance. A state charter law could ensure that charter authorizers have sufficient resources to scrutinize applications and operate charter schools carefully. Furthermore, a structure in which charter-school officials gather and share successes and failures could help meet this goal not only within the charter-school community but in the educational community more generally.

The promising results of the analysis of long-term effects of charter high schools on educational attainment are, for now, available in only two sites, making inferences about policy particularly challenging.

Nonetheless, the findings suggest at least two possibilities for policymakers to consider, with potential relevance for TPSs as well as charter schools. First, the unusual grade-level configurations of many of the charter high schools in Chicago suggest that school-district leaders and charter-school leaders alike might seriously consider eliminating the school transition between middle school and high school (although the positive results seem to hold up for conventionally configured schools as well). The high-school transition is often a difficult one, and the simple strategy of keeping students in the same schools from seventh grade (or earlier) through 12th grade might reduce the dropout rate—perhaps even if the school is not a charter school. Schools with unconventionally long grade configurations are now being created in several urban districts around the country (e.g., New York, Chicago, Philadelphia, and Pittsburgh), and it will be interesting to see whether these district-run schools can replicate the positive attainment effects measured in charter schools that include similar grade configurations. Whether the grade configuration by itself can produce positive effects, in the absence of other features of charter schools, is unknown as yet.

The similarity of the charter attainment results to (some) previous results on Catholic schools also suggests the possible value of seeking to replicate characteristics that charter and Catholic high schools have in common. Some researchers (e.g., Bryk, Lee, and Holland, 1993) have attributed the success of Catholic high schools to their focus on a coherent, pervasive educational mission. We have no data on the extent to which charter high schools exhibit a similarly coherent mission-driven focus, but the ability to create such schools has often been cited by proponents of charters and other varieties of school choice (see, e.g., P. Hill, Foster, and Gendler, 1990; P. Hill, Pierce, and Guthrie, 1997; Whitman, 2008; and Mathews, 2009). The area merits consideration by policymakers and further examination by researchers.

Finally, we turn to the potential policy implications of the analysis of the systemic effects of charter schools on student achievement in nearby TPSs, as presented in Chapter Five. The complete absence of any significant negative effects on TPS students is encouraging and at least suggests that this concern, often voiced by charter-school opponents, may not be justified. But at the same time, the near-complete absence of positive competitive effects (excepting small positive effects estimated in Texas) should be a disappointment to charter-school supporters who hope that healthy competition will induce TPSs to improve. It is possible that our methods are not successfully measuring true competitive effects, but the possibility that charter schools have not, in fact, produced competitive effects is consistent with the predictions of political scientist Frederick Hess (1999 and others), who has extensively chronicled the inability of local school districts to respond productively to competitive pressure. The results of our competition analysis provide some support for Hess's admonition that policymakers should not expect substantial improvements in TPS performance as a result of charter-school competition, in the absence of dramatic changes in the structures, incentives, culture, and operation of conventional school districts.

Methodological and Research Implications

The findings of this study have some clear implications for future research in addition to suggesting promising policy directions. Indeed, future studies of charter schools might benefit not only from the aspects of this study that produced clear findings, but also from the uncertainties identified here.

Some of the implications for future research are particularly relevant for the methods used to estimate charter schools' test-score impacts. First, the findings in Chapter Two related to the characteristics of students entering charter schools cast doubt on the ability of cross-sectional comparisons of charter students and noncharter students to produce valid estimates of charter-school impacts that successfully control for selection bias. Students entering charter schools have baseline scores that often fall short of local average achievement levels, even as compared with others of the same racial group. This suggests that cross-sectional controls for students' observable characteristics might underestimate charter students' baseline achievement disadvantage, leading to an estimate of charter-school impacts that is biased downward.

The longitudinal, quasi-experimental, student fixed-effect method does not emerge from our analysis unscathed, at least for purposes of assessing the impacts of charter elementary schools. Charter schools with entry grades at the middle- and high-school levels are far less subject to the methodological challenges raised by Hoxby and Murarka (2006, 2007). Because all students entering these schools came from other schools, and because all of them are old enough to have been tested in their prior schools, we need not worry that they are different from other (nonswitching) charter students, and there is less reason to believe that their decision to enroll was based on a time-specific event that would have changed their underlying achievement trajectories even if they had not enrolled. For charter schools that begin in kindergarten, however, we have no such reassurance, because impact estimates for those schools are based on the students transferring in later than the entry grades and on those who exit the school for TPSs. In sum, unless and until it is possible to validate the student fixed-effect method with gold-standard experimental results across multiple charter schools, we do not believe that the student fixed-effect method can support strong inferences about the achievement impact of elementary charter schools.[1]

Finally, one of the most important implications of our work for future research on charter schools is the need to move beyond test scores and broaden the scope of measures and questions examined. Our estimates of positive charter-school effects on students' long-term attainment outcomes are more favorable to charters than are most of the test score–based studies to date (including our own test-score results). They suggest that the most important effects of charter schools might not be fully measured in test-score results. But we were able to examine attainment outcomes in only two sites, and it will be important to examine whether charter high schools in other locations are producing similarly favorable outcomes. In addition, follow-up research is needed in Chicago, Florida, and elsewhere to examine what charter high schools are

[1] Mathematica Policy Research is currently engaged in two studies of charter schools that aim to determine whether particular quasi-experimental methods (such as the student fixed-effect method) can reliably replicate experimental impact estimates.

doing to promote higher graduation and college-attendance rates; getting inside the black box will be important for drawing implications that might be relevant to the improvement of TPSs as well as charter schools. Future studies of charter schools should seek to examine a broad and deep range of student outcome measures and to provide evidence on the mechanisms producing positive long-term impacts.

APPENDIX A

Data

In this appendix, we describe location-by-location data provided to us.

Chicago

Chicago Public Schools provided the project team with student-level race and ethnicity information, test-score data, and the school of attendance and grade enrolled for each school year from 1997–98 through 2006–07. The data include Chicago charter schools, and we were able to use the data to calculate how many years each student had attended each charter school. The district also provided school addresses, which were geocoded in order to calculate distances between schools.

The grade range of test scores provided varied by year. For the 1997–98 through 2000–01 school years, math and reading test scores were provided for students in grades 1–8. For 2001–02 through 2006–07, math and reading test scores were provided for students in grades 3–8.

In addition, the district provided student-level data for the educational attainment analysis. These data include all students who attended charter schools in Chicago in eighth grade, whether they attended a traditional public high school or a charter high school. The data cover five cohorts of eighth-grade students, those who began eighth grade from the 1997–98 school year through the 2001–02 school year.

The data include student records for grades 8–12 from the Chicago Public Schools data system, with eighth-grade Iowa Tests of Basic

Skills (ITBS) math and reading scaled scores and information on student gender, race and ethnicity, bilingual status, free or reduced-price lunch status, and special-education status. The data are also linked to the National Student Clearinghouse, which tracks college attendance for students who graduated from the Chicago public school system.

High-school graduation is determined by withdrawal information from the Chicago Public Schools data. Only students who receive a standard high-school diploma are considered to be high-school graduates. For students who leave the Chicago public school system, we impute their graduation status with a regression model as described for Florida. For Chicago, we have college attendance data only for students who graduated from the Chicago public school system, so we also impute college attendance for students with missing graduation data, using the same regression model as for graduation imputation.

Denver

Denver Public Schools provided the project team with student-level race and ethnicity information, test-score data, and the school of attendance and grade enrolled for each school year from 2000–01 through 2005–06. In addition, the district provided a list of school identifiers of each charter school and the year in which the school was established. Using this list combined with the school identifiers for each student, we were able to indicate not only whether a student attended a charter school for each year but also how long the school had been in operation. Using the school identifier for each student, we were able to indicate how many years each student has attended a charter school. Finally, the district also provided school addresses, which were used to geocode the data and determine the distances of each school to every other school.

However, it should be noted that, because a substantial portion of students did not have school identifiers included in the 2000–01 school year, we deleted this year from our analysis and examined data from the 2001–02 through 2006–07 school years only.

The grade range of test scores provided varied across reading and math. For reading, test scores were provided for grades 3 through 10 for each of these years. For math, in the 2001–02 through 2003–04 school years, test scores were provided in grades 5 though 10. In the 2005–06 school year, test scores were provided in grades 3 through 10. We are therefore able to track the student achievement progress more completely in reading than in math.

Florida

The Florida data come from a variety of sources. The primary source for student-level information is the Florida Department of Education's EDW, an integrated longitudinal database covering all public-school students and teachers in the state of Florida. The EDW includes detailed enrollment, demographic, and program-participation information for each student, as well as the students' reading and math achievement test scores.

The EDW includes student records for both K–12 public-school students and students enrolled in community colleges or four-year public universities in Florida. It also contains information on the Florida Resident Access Grant (FRAG), a grant available to Florida residents who attend private colleges and universities in Florida. This effectively allows one to track students who attend private institutions of higher education within Florida. Data from the National Student Clearinghouse, a national database that includes enrollment data on 3,300 colleges throughout the United States, are used to track college attendance outside the state of Florida as well as any private-college enrollment in Florida not picked up by the FRAG data (see National Student Clearinghouse, undated).

The identity and location of schools is determined by the Master School Identification file (for public K–12 schools) and the Nonpublic Master Files (for private schools) maintained by the Florida Department of Education. Grade offerings are determined by enrollment in the October membership survey and by the school grade-configuration information in the relevant school ID file.

High-school graduation is determined by withdrawal information and student-award data from the EDW. Only students who receive a standard high-school diploma are considered to be high-school graduates. Students earning a GED or special-education diploma are counted as not graduating. Similarly, students who withdrew with no intention of returning or exited for other reasons, such as nonattendance, court action, joining the military, marriage, pregnancy, and medical problems, but did not later graduate are counted as not graduating. Students who died while in school are removed from the sample. It is not possible to directly determine the graduation status of students who leave the Florida public school system to attend a homeschooling program or to enroll in a private school or who move out of state. Similarly, some students leave the public school system for unknown reasons. Students whose graduation status is unknown are more likely to have lower eighth-grade test scores and possess other characteristics associated with a reduced likelihood of graduation. They also are more likely to initially attend a traditional high school rather than a charter high school. To avoid possible bias associated with differential sample attrition, we impute the graduation status for those students whose graduation outcome is unknown, based on predicted values from a regression model of graduation. Since we can track college attendance both within and outside of Florida, no imputation is necessary for the college-attendance variable. Any individual who does not show up as enrolled in a two- or four-year college or university is classified as a nonattendee.

The available data cover four cohorts of eighth-grade students. Statewide achievement testing for eighth-grade students began in the 1997–98 school year, so the first cohort in the sample is students who attended eighth grade in 1997–98.[1] The last available year of student data is 2004–05. Given that high-school completion typically takes four years, this means that the last cohort that can be tracked through high school are students who attended grade 8 in 2000–01.

---

1 Data on LEP and special education–program participation begins in 1998–99 and is thus not available for the first eighth-grade cohort. For these students, we use the LEP and special-education status in ninth grade.

Milwaukee

The Milwaukee public school district provided student-level test and demographic data from the 1997–98 through 2006–07 school years. During the course of the panel, state tests switched from the TerraNova to the Wisconsin Knowledge Concepts Examination (WKCE), which, in the past few years, has incorporated ever more state-developed items. Therefore, to enable us to measure student gain scores, we created z-scores using scale scores by year, grade level, and test subject.

We could not use all of the data that the district provided for a number of reasons, however. First, the data from 1997–1999 were too sparse to estimate gain scores, so we limited the analyses to the 2000–01 through 2006–07 school years. Second, although the district provided test data for students in grades 2–10 in math and reading, there were too many missing scores in grade 2 to estimate the models. Therefore, we focused the analyses on math and reading achievement in grades 3–10, which provides us with gain scores for grades 4–10. Third, we obtained data for only those charter schools that the Milwaukee public school system chartered (which comprise the majority of charter schools in Milwaukee) and therefore were unable to incorporate into this study schools chartered by other entities (i.e., independent charter schools). Finally, it is important to note that the data we analyzed include tested students only.

Ohio

The State of Ohio provided us with student-level race information, test-score data, and school of attendance and grade enrolled from year 2003–04 through 2007–08. However, these variables were not provided for all students for each year, but the subset of students tested in the particular year. In addition, which grades were tested varied by year. Also, in some years, students were tested in the fall. Because a small portion of students were actually tested in the fall and because it would have meant that we would not have consistent intervals of testing periods for all students, we eliminated the fall test. Furthermore, in the 2003–04 school year, only third graders were tested in reading, and no students were tested in math. Also, only a portion of third graders were tested in reading in the 2003–04 school year. Therefore, we also eliminated all 2003–04 school-year data from our analysis.

We also performed several checks on the data and dropped records outside of our population as well as records that had conflicting information. In the first cut of the data, we removed all records for subjects other than math and reading. We dropped all records for a student in math and reading if the student had more than two records for a single subject. In total, we dropped less than 2 percent of students in each year by selecting out our population and discarding student records with conflicting data. As noted, in some cases, the research team was given both spring and fall test results for an individual student. Of the students with two records in a subject in a year, we kept a single student record for each subject when information on the student was consistent and dropped both student records when the data were incongruent. We dropped both records if (1) gender, race, or school was discrepant; (2) we had two different spring scores or two different fall scores for a student; or (3) neither record had school data. We dropped inconsistent student records across math and reading within a year—when gender, race, or school did not match—and we dropped student records with inconsistent gender data across years.

In the 2004–05 school year, the state provided math test scores in grades 3, 7, and 8 and reading test scores in grades 3, 4, 5, and 8. In the 2005–06 through 2007–08 school years, the state provided reading test scores for grades 3 through 8. It should also be noted that, for many students, the state provided both raw scores and scaled scores. However, we had only the raw or scaled scores (not both) for a small subset of students. To maximize the scores, we normalized the raw and scaled scores by year and grade. For students missing scaled normalized scores, we used the raw normalized values. It should be noted that the raw and scaled scores had a high correlation of 0.87 across students who had both scores.

Philadelphia

The School District of Philadelphia provided the project team with student-level race and ethnicity information, test-score data, and the school of attendance and grade enrolled for each school year from 2000–01 through 2006–07. In addition, the district provided a list of school identifiers of each charter school and the year in which the school was established. Using this list combined with the school identifiers for each student, we were able to identify not only whether a student attended a charter school for each year but also how long the school had been in operation. Using the school identifier for each student, we were able to indicate how many years each student has attended a charter school. Finally, the district also provided school addresses, which were used to geocode the data and determine the distances of each school to every other school.

In the period under examination (2000–01 through 2006–07), students in Philadelphia took three kinds of annual achievement tests in reading and math, varying with the school year and grade:

- Pennsylvania System of School Assessment (PSSA) tests for math and reading for grades 5, 8, and 11 annually beginning in spring 2001 and grades 3 through 8 and 11 in spring 2006 and 2007
- Stanford Achievement Test Series, Ninth Edition (Stanford 9), tests in math and reading in grades 3, 4, 7, and 10 in spring 2001 and spring 2002[2]
- TerraNova tests in math in grades 2 through 10 annually in the springs of 2003 through 2005 and in grades 2, 9, and 10 in spring 2006
- TerraNova tests in reading in grades 1 through 10 annually in the springs of 2003 through 2005 and in grades 1, 2, 9, and 10 in spring 2006.

---

[2] In the spring of 2002, the Stanford 9 fourth-grade test was administered only to K–4 schools and not to K–5 or K–8 schools (email correspondence with Michael Schlesinger, director of accountability, School District of Philadelphia, February 16, 2008).

Although we were able to get the Stanford 9 test results for non-charter students in 2001 and 2002, we were unable to get these data for charter students. However, it is still valuable to have these data in these years because they can help track the performance of students who later enrolled in charter schools.

Because there is no consistent scale across the various tests on which to gauge absolute changes in student achievement over time, we convert all scaled test-score results into rank-based z-scores, by year and grade, with a mean of 0 and a standard deviation of 1. Specifically, we sort all student scores by rank and then convert them to z-scores that are normed across the entire districtwide population of tested students in that subject and grade. This conversion does not require that students have the same rank on one test as on another, but it assumes that differences in the distribution of students on different tests are not correlated with charter status. Random differences in student ranks across different tests would introduce noise, but not bias, to the analysis. The conversion of scaled scores to rank-based z-scores means that we cannot make claims about the absolute amount of learning in one school or another (lacking a psychometrically valid developmental scale), but it permits an examination of changes in rank with fewer assumptions than would be needed under other kinds of scaling.[3] In cases in which students took both the TerraNova and PSSA, we used the PSSA because it is the state accountability measure and, in recent years, has been administered in more grades.[4]

---

[3] For further discussion of the use of rank-based z-scores, see Gill, Hamilton, et al. (2005).

[4] The PSSA is the state accountability test and therefore can be considered a high-stakes test. By contrast, the TerraNova and Stanford 9, which are nationally normed tests, may be considered low-stakes measures in Philadelphia because there are no direct consequences for students or educators based on performance. There are advantages and disadvantages to using scores from state accountability tests for evaluations such as this one. Because these tests are developed to be aligned with state content standards, they may be more likely than other measures to reflect the educational goals of the schools in that state. However, there is ample evidence that high-stakes tests lead to instructional changes that can inflate scores and that gains on these tests do not always generalize to other tests that are intended to measure the same outcomes (Hamilton, 2003). In the past, when one test is not administered in

San Diego

The San Diego Unified School District provided the project team with student-level race and ethnicity information, test-score data, an indicator of whether the student attends a charter school, and the school of attendance and grade enrolled for each school year from 1997–98 through 2006–07. We also collected information from the California State Department of Education (undated) to determine the start date of schools and longitudes and latitudes, which were used to geocode the data and determine the distances of each school to every other school.[5] For each school year and for both reading and math, test scores of students were provided in grades 2 through 11.

Texas

The State of Texas provided the project team with student-level race information, test-score data, and school of attendance and grade enrolled from 1995–96 through 2003–04. These data include math and reading test scores for students in grades 3–8 in all years for all public-school students, including students in Texas charter schools. Using these data along with school identifiers, we were able to follow each student over time as he or she transitioned between schools, and determine how many years each student attended a charter school. The data also included geocode information, which we used to determine distances between schools.

For 2001–02 and prior school years, the test scores were the math and reading scaled scores on the Texas Assessment of Academic Skills (TAAS), and, for 2002–03 and 2003–04, the test scores were the math and reading scaled scores on the Texas Assessment of Knowledge and

---

consecutive grades across years, researchers have often combine high- and low-stakes tests to track performance of students over time (May, Supovitz, and Perda, 2004).

5 For a limited set of schools, latitudes and longitudes were unavailable on the state Web sites. Therefore, we looked up the addresses of these schools on other Web sites to create the longitudes and latitudes for these schools.

Skills (TAKS). Because these tests are on different scales, we converted all scores to rank-based z-scores, by year, test, and grade.

APPENDIX B

Chapter Three Regression Results

In this appendix, we provide a more-detailed description of the regression results, including sample size, the values for the R-squared, and estimates for control variables. For the sake of space, we have excluded the coefficient and standard error estimate for the grade-by-year interactions.

Table B.1
Detailed Initial Math Results for Table 3.1

Variable	Chicago	Denver	Milwaukee	Philadelphia	San Diego	Ohio	Texas
Charter estimate	0.02 (0.02)	0.17** (0.06)	0.05* (0.02)	−0.03 (0.02)	0.02 (0.02)	−0.18* (0.04)	−0.12** (0.02)
Transferring to a new school	−0.03* (0.01)	−0.05* (0.02)	−0.08** (0.01)	−0.10** (0.01)	−0.06** (0.01)	−0.05** (0.01)	−0.13** (0.01)
Observations	1,195,923	85,162	237,308	547,405	676,148	1,523,597	1,260,655
R-squared	0.24	0.47	0.22	0.26	0.17	0.46	0.17

NOTE: Each model includes a set of year-by-grade indicators. Standard errors, adjusted for the clustering of students within schools, are in parentheses. * = statistically significant at the 5-percent level. ** = statistically significant at the 1-percent level.

Table B.2
Detailed Initial Reading Results for Table 3.1

Variable	Chicago	Denver	Milwaukee	Philadelphia	San Diego	Ohio	Texas
Overall estimate	−0.04** (0.01)	0.04 (0.03)	0.01 (0.01)	−0.03 (0.02)	0.01 (0.01)	−0.08** (0.02)	−0.08** (0.01)
Transferring to a new school	−0.01 (0.01)	−0.03* (0.01)	−0.05** (0.01)	−0.08** (0.01)	−0.04** (0.01)	−0.05** (0.01)	−0.09** (0.01)
Observations	1,199,776	113,257	221,258	582,889	676,731	1,643,489	1,252,621
R-squared	0.20	0.35	0.23	0.22	0.18	0.33	0.17

NOTE: Each model includes a set of year-by-grade indicators. Standard errors, adjusted for the clustering of students within schools, are in parentheses. * = statistically significant at the 5-percent level. ** = statistically significant at the 1-percent level.

Table B.3
Detailed Math Results for Students Always in Charter Schools Relative to Students Who Transfer Between Charter Schools and Traditional Public Schools in Table 3.2

Variable	Chicago	Denver	Milwaukee	Philadelphia	San Diego	Ohio	Texas
Achievement gains of students always in a charter school	0.03* (0.01)	−0.03 (0.05)	−0.01 (0.02)	0.03** (0.01)	0.00 (0.02)	0.09** (0.03)	0.16** (0.02)
Observations	42,542	8,436	59,101	97,949	105,904	79,416	82,961
R-squared	0.02	0.08	0.03	0.02	0.02	0.08	0.08

NOTE: Standard errors, adjusted for the clustering of students within schools, are in parentheses. * = statistically significant at the 5-percent level. ** = statistically significant at the 1-percent level.

Table B.4
Detailed Reading Results for Students Always in Charter Schools Relative to Students Who Transfer Between Charter Schools and Traditional Public Schools in Table 3.2

Variable	Chicago	Denver	Milwaukee	Philadelphia	San Diego	Ohio	Texas
Achievement gains of students always in a charter school	0.02 (0.01)	0.03 (0.04)	0.01 (0.01)	0.01 (0.01)	0.00 (0.01)	0.06** (0.02)	0.10** (0.01)
Observations	42,571	11,290	54,767	103,703	106,337	90,342	82,483
R-squared	0.01	0.03	0.01	0.01	0.01	0.05	0.06

NOTE: Standard errors, adjusted for the clustering of students within schools, are in parentheses. * = statistically significant at the 5-percent level. ** = statistically significant at the 1-percent level.

Table B.5
Detailed Math Results for Nonprimary Charter Schools in Table 3.3

Variable	Chicago	Denver	Milwaukee	Philadelphia	San Diego	Ohio	Texas
Restricted sample estimate	−0.06 (0.04)	0.10 (0.06)	0.03 (0.02)	−0.02 (0.03)	0.01 (0.02)	−0.01 (0.07)	−0.08* (0.02)
Transferring to a new school	−0.03* (0.01)	−0.05* (0.02)	−0.08** (0.01)	−0.10** (0.02)	−0.06** (0.01)	−0.05** (0.01)	−0.09** (0.01)
Observations	1,175,067	81,793	241,076	512,980	665,361	1,476,865	1,235,427
R-squared	0.24	0.47	0.21	0.27	0.17	0.47	0.17

NOTE: Each model includes a set of year-by-grade indicators. Standard errors, adjusted for the clustering of students within schools, are in parentheses. * = statistically significant at the 5-percent level. ** = statistically significant at the 1-percent level.

Table B.6
Detailed Reading Results for Nonprimary Charter Schools in Table 3.3

Variable	Chicago	Denver	Milwaukee	Philadelphia	San Diego	Ohio	Texas
Restricted sample estimate	−0.09** (0.02)	0.03 (0.03)	0.00 (0.01)	−0.01 (0.02)	0.02 (0.02)	0.00 (0.05)	−0.08** (0.04)
Transferring to a new school	−0.01 (0.01)	−0.03* (0.01)	−0.06** (0.01)	−0.08** (0.01)	−0.04** (0.01)	−0.05** (0.01)	−0.13** (0.01)
Observations	1,178,862	109,156	213,464	544,089	666,061	1,592,472	1,227,432
R-squared	0.21	0.36	0.24	0.22	0.18	0.33	0.22

NOTE: Each model includes a set of year-by-grade indicators. Standard errors, adjusted for the clustering of students within schools, are in parentheses. * = statistically significant at the 5-percent level. ** = statistically significant at the 1-percent level.

Table B.7
Detailed Math and Reading Results for Ohio Virtual and Classroom-Based Charter Schools in Table 3.4

Variable	Math		Reading	
Virtual schools for all grades	−0.44** (0.04)		−0.25** (0.03)	
Classroom-based schools for all grades	−0.05 (0.03)		−0.01 (0.02)	
Virtual schools, restricting the sample of schools to upper grades		−0.65** (0.25)		−0.13 (0.24)
Classroom-based schools, restricting the sample of schools to upper grades		0.00 (0.07)		0.00 (0.05)
Transferring to a new school	−0.05** (0.01)	−0.05** 0.01)	−0.05** (0.01)	−0.05** (0.01)
Observations	1,523,597	1,476,865	1,643,489	1,592,472
R-squared	0.46	0.47	0.33	0.33

NOTE: Each model includes a set of year-by-grade indicators. Standard errors, adjusted for the clustering of students within schools, are in parentheses. * = statistically significant at the 5-percent level. ** = statistically significant at the 1-percent level.

Table B.8
Detailed Math Results, by Age of Charter Schools, for Table 3.5

Variable	Chicago	Denver	Milwaukee	Philadelphia	San Diego	Ohio	Texas
Charter school in 1st year of operation	−0.24** (0.06)	0.25* (0.10)	−0.02 (0.04)	−0.01 (0.08)	0.01 (0.08)	−0.30** (0.12)	−0.22** (0.04)
Charter school in 2nd year of operation	−0.04 (0.05)	0.13 (0.13)	0.04 (0.04)	−0.01 (0.04)	0.02 (0.05)	−0.23** (0.06)	−0.10** (0.03)
Charter school in 3rd year of operation	0.06** (0.01)	0.16 (0.09)	0.05 (0.03)	−0.04 (0.02)	0.02 (0.02)	−0.17** (0.04)	−0.08** (0.02)
Transferring to a new school	−0.03* (0.01)	−0.05* (0.02)	−0.08** (0.01)	−0.10** (0.01)	−0.06** (0.01)	−0.05** (0.01)	−0.13** (0.01)
Observations	1,195,923	85,162	237,308	547,373	676,148	1,523,597	1,260,665
R-squared	0.24	0.47	0.22	0.26	0.17	0.46	0.17

NOTE: Each model includes a set of year-by-grade indicators. Standard errors, adjusted for the clustering of students within schools, are in parentheses. * = statistically significant at the 5-percent level. ** = statistically significant at the 1-percent level.

Table B.9
Detailed Reading Results, by Age of Charter Schools, for Table 3.5

Variable	Chicago	Denver	Milwaukee	Philadelphia	San Diego	Ohio	Texas
Charter school in 1st year of operation	−0.11** (0.02)	0.01 (0.04)	0.00 (0.02)	0.02 (0.05)	0.00 (0.03)	−0.17 (0.09)	−0.14** (0.03)
Charter school in 2nd year of operation	−0.04 (0.03)	0.03 (0.04)	−0.01 (0.02)	−0.04 (0.03)	0.01 (0.02)	−0.13** (0.04)	−0.11** (0.02)
Charter school in 3rd year of operation	−0.03 (0.01)	0.05 (0.04)	0.01 (0.01)	−0.03 (0.02)	0.02 (0.02)	−0.07* (0.03)	−0.04** (0.01)
Transferring to a new school	−0.01 (0.01)	−0.03* (0.01)	−0.05** (0.01)	−0.08** (0.01)	−0.04** (0.01)	−0.05** (0.01)	−0.09** (0.01)
Observations	1,199,776	113,257	221,258	582,877	676,731	1,643,489	1,252,621
R-squared	0.21	0.35	0.23	0.22	0.18	0.33	0.17

NOTE: Each model includes a set of year-by-grade indicators. Standard errors, adjusted for the clustering of students within schools, are in parentheses. * = statistically significant at the 5-percent level. ** = statistically significant at the 1-percent level.

Table B.10
Detailed Math Results, by Race and Ethnicity, for Table 3.6

Variable	Chicago	Denver	Milwaukee	Philadelphia	San Diego	Ohio	Texas
African American students	0.02 (0.03)	0.13 (0.08)	0.02 (0.02)	−0.04 (0.03)	0.05 (0.03)	0.06 (0.09)	−0.03 (0.06)
Hispanic students	−0.14** (0.04)	0.07 (0.07)	0.05 (0.03)	0.04 (0.05)	0.00 (0.04)	0.08 (0.21)	−0.10* (0.05)
White students	−0.08 (0.13)	0.23** (0.06)	0.03 (0.03)	0.04 (0.03)	0.01 (0.03)	−0.10 (0.07)	−0.14** (0.04)
Other students	−0.27** (0.05)	−0.01 (0.11)	−0.01 (0.04)	0.01 (0.07)	0.01 (0.02)	0.00 (0.24)	−0.11 (0.14)
Transferring to a new school	−0.03* (0.01)	−0.05* (0.02)	−0.08** (0.01)	−0.10** (0.02)	−0.06** (0.01)	−0.05** (0.01)	−0.13** (0.01)
Observations	1,175,058	81,793	229,668	512,980	664,522	1,462,726	1,235,427
R-squared	0.24	0.47	0.22	0.27	0.17	0.47	0.17

NOTE: Each model includes a set of year-by-grade indicators. Standard errors, adjusted for the clustering of students within schools, are in parentheses. * = statistically significant at the 5-percent level. ** = statistically significant at the 1-percent level.

Table B.11
Detailed Reading Results, by Race and Ethnicity, for Table 3.6

Variable	Chicago	Denver	Milwaukee	Philadelphia	San Diego	Ohio	Texas
African American students	−0.04 (0.03)	0.01 (0.05)	0.00 (0.01)	−0.01 (0.03)	0.05** (0.01)	0.04 (0.07)	−0.08* (0.04)
Hispanic students	−0.14** (0.02)	0.05 (0.03)	0.00 (0.02)	0.02 (0.03)	0.01 (0.02)	−0.13 (0.13)	−0.08* (0.03)
White students	−0.09 (0.08)	−0.08 (0.07)	0.03 (0.02)	0.03 (0.03)	0.03 (0.03)	0.01 (0.07)	−0.10* (0.04)
Other students	−0.24** (0.03)	0.01 (0.09)	−0.01 (0.02)	0.02 (0.09)	−0.01 (0.02)	0.14 (0.18)	0.16 (0.19)
Transferring to a new school	−0.01 (0.01)	−0.03* (0.01)	−0.06** (0.01)	−0.08** (0.01)	−0.04** (0.01)	−0.05** (0.01)	−0.09** (0.01)
Observations	1,178,853	109,156	214,572	544,089	665,217	1,575,425	1,227,529
R-squared	0.21	0.36	0.24	0.23	0.18	0.33	0.17

NOTE: Each model includes a set of year-by-grade indicators. Standard errors, adjusted for the clustering of students within schools, are in parentheses. * = statistically significant at the 5-percent level. ** = statistically significant at the 1-percent level.

APPENDIX C

Supporting Data

Table C.1
Tenth-Grade Location, by Type of Transition Between Eighth and Ninth Grades

	Florida				Chicago			
	To Traditional		To Charter		To Traditional		To Charter	
Variable	Obs.	Mean	Obs.	Mean	Obs.	Mean	Obs.	Mean
Enrolled in TPS in G10	2,084	0.962	1,144	0.167	425	0.984	408	0.177
Enrolled in charter school in G10	2,084	0.038	1,144	0.833	425	0.016	408	0.823

Table C.2
Probit Estimates of Receiving a Standard High-School Diploma (coefficient estimates are marginal effects), Sample Restricted to Students Who Were in the Same Type of School (traditional or charter) in Both Ninth and 10th Grades

	Florida		Chicago
Variable	Within 4 Years	Within 5 Years	Within 5+ Years
Attend charter HS	0.1253*** (0.0320)	0.1472*** (0.0379)	0.0535 (0.0324)
Math score, G8	0.0033*** (0.0003)	0.0036*** (0.0005)	0.0007 (0.0008)
Reading score, G8	0.0020*** (0.0003)	0.0017*** (0.0003)	0.0022*** (0.0006)
Female	0.0604*** (0.0165)	0.0386 (0.0286)	0.0874*** (0.0331)
African American	0.0416** (0.0199)	0.0908*** (0.0324)	0.0180 (0.1069)
Hispanic	0.0972*** (0.0282)	0.1132** (0.0441)	−0.0902 (0.1476)
Asian	0.0833 (0.0894)	0.1286 (0.1154)	
LEP/bilingual, G8	0.0491 (0.0918)	0.0327 (0.1554)	0.0318 (0.0817)
Special ed, G8	0.0955*** (0.0314)	0.0929** (0.0394)	0.0514 (0.0440)
Free/reduced-price lunch, G8	−0.1660*** (0.0254)	−0.1216*** (0.0339)	0.0150 (0.0524)
Changed schools, G7 or G8	−0.0703*** (0.0259)	−0.0115 (0.0373)	−0.0475 (0.0343)
Observations	3,410	1,686	741

NOTE: Each model includes a set of cohort indicators. Standard errors, adjusted for clustering at the school level, are in parentheses. ** = statistically significant at the 5-percent level. *** = statistically significant at the 1-percent level.

Table C.3
Probit Estimates of Attending a Two-Year or Four-Year College Within Five Years (coefficient estimates are marginal effects), Sample Restricted to Students Who Were in the Same Type of School (traditional or charter) in Both Ninth and 10th Grades

Variable	Florida	Chicago
Attend charter HS	0.0899*** (0.0295)	0.1007 (0.0621)
Math score, G8	0.0012*** (0.0005)	0.0022 (0.0014)
Reading score, G8	0.0024*** (0.0004)	0.0026** (0.0010)
Female	0.0917*** (0.0298)	0.1156** (0.0425)
African American	0.0527 (0.0378)	0.0446 (0.1397)
Hispanic	0.1801*** (0.0544)	−0.1932 (0.1295)
Asian	0.2727** (0.1029)	
LEP/bilingual, G8	−0.2907** (0.0865)	0.1899** (0.0964)
Special ed, G8	0.0445 (0.0459)	−0.0703 (0.0756)
Free/reduced-price lunch, G8	−0.1504*** (0.0262)	0.0215 (0.0826)
Changed schools, G7 or G8	−0.0427 (0.0319)	−0.0172 (0.0541)
Observations	1,688	509

NOTE: Each model includes a set of cohort indicators. Standard errors, adjusted for clustering at the school level, are in parentheses. ** = statistically significant at the 5-percent level. *** = statistically significant at the 1-percent level.

Table C.4
Ordinary Least Squares Estimates of the Determinants of 10th-Grade Achievement-Test Scores

	Florida		Chicago	
Variable	**Math**	**Reading**	**Math**	**Reading**
Attend charter HS	–3.0140* (1.7176)	1.9708 (1.8656)	0.2743* (0.1478)	0.5533** (0.2191)
Math score, G8	0.6502*** (0.0205)		0.0791*** (0.0038)	
Reading score, G8		0.6508*** (0.0206)		0.0969*** (0.0047)
Female	–5.6823*** (0.8848)	–0.6120 (1.2690)	–0.0842 (0.0946)	0.4754** (0.1951)
African American	–9.0295*** (1.7447)	–9.5340*** (1.6819)	–1.1637* (0.6078)	–1.6731** (0.7792)
Hispanic	0.1169 (1.3359)	–0.4565 (1.5311)	–0.4299 (0.6537)	–0.7337 (0.8574)
Asian	3.1367 (3.1829)	–7.8507** (3.9892)	0.6942 (0.6148)	–2.6232*** (0.7854)
LEP/bilingual, G8	–1.5450 (2.4511)	1.6469 (11.3321)	–0.4468 (0.2847)	–0.7117 (0.6484)
Special ed, G8	–6.4861** (2.6886)	–11.3290*** (2.9600)	0.3093 (0.2149)	–0.4412 (0.3454)
Free/reduced-price lunch, G8	–3.4854** (1.4957)	–4.4255*** (1.5441)	–0.7776*** (0.2581)	–0.2601 (0.3533)
Changed schools, G7 or G8	–1.0068 (1.1078)	0.5110 (1.3150)	–0.2789* (0.1638)	–0.0908 (0.1943)
R-squared	0.712	0.601	0.550	0.485
Observations	2,465	2,471	978	978

NOTE: Each model includes a set of cohort indicators. Standard errors, adjusted for clustering at the school level, are in parentheses. * = statistically significant at the 10-percent level. ** = statistically significant at the 5-percent level. *** = statistically significant at the 1-percent level.

Table C.5
Two-Stage Least Squares Estimates of the Determinants of 10th-Grade Achievement-Test Scores

	Florida		Chicago	
Variable	**Math**	**Reading**	**Math**	**Reading**
Attend charter HS	1.0020 (3.1050)	1.9657 (2.8143)	0.7806*** (0.2708)	0.4873 (0.4687)
Math score, G8	0.6493*** (0.0205)		0.0807*** (0.0043)	
Reading score, G8		0.6508*** (0.0205)		0.0968*** (0.0048)
Female	–5.6529*** (0.8747)	–0.6200 (1.2656)	–0.1091 (0.0998)	0.4789** (0.1969)
African American	–8.6800*** (1.7814)	–9.5134*** (1.6507)	–1.1813* (0.6498)	–1.6694** (0.7842)
Hispanic	–0.1882 (1.4034)	–0.4592 (1.5240)	–0.4824 (0.6761)	–0.7277 (0.8591)
Asian	2.8318 (3.3794)	–7.8449** (3.9589)	0.9546 (0.6579)	–2.6561*** (0.8192)
LEP/bilingual, G8	–1.5323 (2.5704)	1.6382 (11.2726)	–0.4474 (0.2811)	–0.7112 (0.6473)
Special ed, G8	–6.1555** (2.6784)	–11.2703*** (2.9565)	0.3861* (0.2105)	–0.4495 (0.3661)
Free/reduced-price lunch, G8	–2.9132** (1.5068)	–4.4142*** (1.4347)	–0.7649*** (0.2665)	–0.2617 (0.3506)
Changed schools, G7 or G8	–1.3260 (1.4901)	0.5247 (1.3708)	–0.2937* (0.1604)	–0.0900 (0.1920)
R-squared	0.710	0.600	0.544	0.484
Observations	2,464	2,470	978	978

NOTE: Each model includes a set of cohort indicators. Standard errors, adjusted for clustering at the school level, are in parentheses. * = statistically significant at the 10-percent level. ** = statistically significant at the 5-percent level. *** = statistically significant at the 1-percent level.

APPENDIX D

Chapter Five Regression Results

In this appendix, we provide a more-detailed description of the regression results for competitive analysis, including sample size and the values for the R-squared.

Table D.1
Detailed Math Results for Competitive Analysis Using Proximity to Charter Schools as a Proxy for Competition in Table 5.1

Variable	Chicago	Denver	Milwaukee	Philadelphia	San Diego	Ohio	Texas
Distance to nearest charter school	0.00 (0.01)	0.03 (0.02)	−0.02 (0.02)	0.01 (0.06)	0.00 (0.01)	0.00 (0.00)	0.00 (0.00)
Observations	1,121,738	80,214	213,773	478,049	625,999	1,435,095	945,092
R-squared	0.46	0.64	0.46	0.50	0.39	0.64	0.50

NOTE: Each model includes a set of year-by-grade indicators. Standard errors, adjusted for the clustering of students within schools, are in parentheses.

Table D.2
Detailed Reading Results for Competitive Analysis Using Proximity to Charter Schools as a Proxy for Competition in Table 5.1

Variable	Chicago	Denver	Milwaukee	Philadelphia	San Diego	Ohio	Texas
Distance to nearest charter school	−0.01 (0.01)	0.01 (0.01)	0.01 (0.02)	0.06 (0.05)	0.01 (0.01)	0.00 (0.00)	0.00 (0.00)
Observations	1,125,394	106,877	192,647	509,140	625,956	1,547,969	938,066
R-squared	0.43	0.59	0.53	0.44	0.40	0.57	0.48

NOTE: Each model includes a set of year-by-grade indicators. Standard errors, adjusted for the clustering of students within schools, are in parentheses.

Table D.3
Detailed Math Results for Competitive Analysis Using Number of Charter Schools Within 2.5 Miles as a Proxy for Competition in Table 5.1

Variable	Chicago	Denver	Milwaukee	Philadelphia	San Diego	Ohio	Texas
Number of charter schools within 2.5 miles	0.01 (0.02)	0.00 (0.04)	0.00 (0.01)	0.01 (0.02)	−0.01 (0.01)	−0.02 (0.02)	0.03* (0.01)
Observations	1,121,738	80,214	213,773	478,049	625,999	1,476,127	1,199,938
R-squared	0.46	0.63	0.49	0.50	0.39	0.64	0.48

NOTE: Each model includes a set of year-by-grade indicators. Standard errors, adjusted for the clustering of students within schools, are in parentheses. * = statistically significant at the 5-percent level.

Table D.4
Detailed Reading Results for Competitive Analysis Using Number of Charter Schools Within 2.5 Miles as a Proxy for Competition in Table 5.1

Variable	Chicago	Denver	Milwaukee	Philadelphia	San Diego	Ohio	Texas
Number of charter schools within 2.5 miles	0.02 (0.01)	0.01 (0.03)	0.00 (0.01)	0.00 (0.01)	0.00 (0.01)	0.02 (0.01)	0.02* (0.01)
Observations	1,125,394	106,877	192,647	509,140	625,956	1,591,688	1,193,323
R-squared	0.43	0.59	0.53	0.44	0.40	0.57	0.460

NOTE: Each model includes a set of year-by-grade indicators. Standard errors, adjusted for the clustering of students within schools, are in parentheses. * = statistically significant at the 5-percent level.

Bibliography

Abdulkadiroglu, Atila, Josh Angrist, Sarah Cohodes, Susan Dynarski, Jon Fullerton, Thomas Kane, and Parag Pathak, *Informing the Debate: Comparing Boston's Charter, Pilot and Traditional Schools*, Boston, Mass.: Boston Foundation, January 2009. As of February 4, 2009:
http://www.tbf.org/uploadedFiles/tbforg/Utility_Navigation/Multimedia_Library/Reports/InformingTheDebate_Final.pdf

Altonji, Joseph G., Todd E. Elder, and Christopher R. Taber, "Selection on Observed and Unobserved Variables: Assessing the Effectiveness of Catholic Schools," *Journal of Political Economy*, Vol. 113, No. 1, February 2005, pp. 151–184.

Arellano, Manuel, and Stephen Bond, "Some Tests of Specification for Panel Data: Monte Carlo Evidence and an Application to Employment Fluctuations," *Review of Economic Studies*, Vol. 58, No. 2, April 1991, pp. 277–197.

Ballou, Dale, Bettie Teasley, and Tim Zeidner, "Charter Schools in Idaho," in Mark Berends, Matthew G. Springer, and Herbert J. Walberg, eds., *Charter School Outcomes*, New York: L. Erlbaum Associates, 2007, pp. 221–241.

Bettinger, Eric P., "The Effect of Charter Schools on Charter Students and Public Schools," *Economics of Education Review*, Vol. 24, No. 2, April 2005, pp. 133–147.

Betts, Julian R., and Paul Thomas Hill, *Key Issues in Studying Charter Schools and Achievement: A Review and Suggestions for National Guidelines*, Seattle, Wash.: Center on Reinventing Public Education, Daniel J. Evans School of Public Affairs, University of Washington, National Charter School Research Project white paper 2, May 2006. As of February 4, 2009:
http://www.uscharterschools.org/cs/r/view/uscs_rs/2177

Betts, Julian R., Loren A. Rice, Andrew C. Zau, Y. Emily Tang, and Cory R. Koedel, *Does School Choice Work? Effects on Student Integration and Achievement*, San Francisco, Calif.: Public Policy Institute of California, 2006. As of February 4, 2009:
http://www.ppic.org/content/pubs/report/R_806JBR.pdf

Betts, Julian R., Y. Emily Tang, and Andrew C. Zau, *Madness in the Method? A Critical Analysis of Popular Methods of Estimating the Effect of Charter Schools on Student Achievement*, delivered at the Annual Meetings of the American Educational Research Association, Chicago, Ill., April 2006.

Bifulco, Robert, and Helen F. Ladd, "The Impacts of Charter Schools on Student Achievement: Evidence from North Carolina," *Education Finance and Policy*, Vol. 1, No. 1, Winter 2006, pp. 50–90. As of February 4, 2009: http://www.mitpressjournals.org/doi/pdf/10.1162/edfp.2006.1.1.50

———, "School Choice, Racial Segregation, and Test-Score Gaps: Evidence from North Carolina's Charter School Program," *Journal of Policy Analysis and Management*, Vol. 26, No. 1, 2007, pp. 31–56.

Booker, Kevin, Brian Gill, Ron Zimmer, and Tim R. Sass, *Achievement and Attainment in Chicago Charter Schools*, Santa Monica, Calif.: RAND Corporation, TR-585-BMG/JOY/SRF/STRF/WPF, 2008. As of February 4, 2009: http://www.rand.org/pubs/technical_reports/TR585/

Booker, Kevin, Scott Gilpatric, Timothy Gronberg, and Dennis Jansen, *The Effect of Charter Schools on Traditional Public School Students in Texas: Are Children Who Stay Behind Left Behind?* New York: National Center for the Study of Privatization in Education, Teachers College, Columbia University, occasional paper 104, September 2005. As of February 5, 2009: http://www.ncspe.org/publications_files/OP104.pdf

———, "The Impact of Charter School Student Attendance on Student Performance," *Journal of Public Economics*, Vol. 91, Nos. 5–6, June 2007, pp. 849–876.

Booker, Kevin, Ron Zimmer, and Richard Buddin, *The Effects of Charter Schools on School Peer Composition*, Santa Monica, Calif.: RAND Corporation, WR-306-EDU, 2005. As of November 5, 2008: http://www.rand.org/pubs/working_papers/WR306/

Bryk, Anthony S., Valerie E. Lee, and Peter Blakeley Holland, *Catholic Schools and the Common Good*, Cambridge, Mass.: Harvard University Press, 1993.

Buddin, Richard, and Ron Zimmer, "A Closer Look at Charter School Student Achievement," *Journal of Policy Analysis and Management*, Vol. 24, No. 2, 2005, pp. 351–372.

———, "Is Charter School Competition in California Improving the Performance of Traditional Public Schools?" *Public Administration Review*, forthcoming.

California State Department of Education, "California School Directory," undated database. As of February 5, 2009: http://www.cde.ca.gov/re/sd/

Catterall, J. S., *Different Ways of Knowing: 1991–94 National Longitudinal Study, Program Effects on Students and Teachers (Final Report)*, Los Angeles, Calif.: University of California, Los Angeles, Graduate School of Education and Information Studies, 1995.

Cohen, Jacob, *Statistical Power Analysis for the Behavioral Sciences*, New York: Academic Press, 1969.

Darling-Hammond, Linda, "Policy and Professionalism," in Ann Lieberman, ed., *Building a Professional Culture in Schools*, New York: Teachers College Press, Teachers College, Columbia University, 1988, pp. 57–77.

———, "Policy for Restructuring," in Ann Lieberman, ed., *The Work of Restructuring Schools: Building from the Ground Up*, New York: Teachers College Press, Teachers College, Columbia University, 1995, pp. 157–175.

———, *The Right to Learn: A Blueprint for Creating Schools That Work*, San Francisco, Calif.: Jossey-Bass, 1997.

Evans, William N., and Robert M. Schwab, "Finishing High School and Starting College: Do Catholic Schools Make a Difference?" *Quarterly Journal of Economics*, Vol. 110, No. 4, November 1995, pp. 941–974.

Frankenberg, Erica, and Chungmei Lee, "Charter Schools and Race: A Lost Opportunity for Integrated Education," *Education Policy Analysis Archives*, Vol. 11, No. 32, September 5, 2003. As of November 5, 2008:
http://epaa.asu.edu/epaa/v11n32/

Fullan, Michael, *Change Forces: The Sequel*, London, UK: Falmer Press, 1999.

Fullan, Michael, and Matthew B. Miles, "Getting Reform Right: What Works and What Doesn't," *Phi Delta Kappan*, Vol. 73, No. 10, 1992, pp. 744–752.

Fullan, Michael, and Suzanne M. Stiegelbauer, *The New Meaning of Educational Change*, 2nd ed., Toronto, Ont.: Ontario Institute for Studies in Education, 1991.

Gill, Brian, Laura S. Hamilton, J. R. Lockwood, Julie A. Marsh, Ron Zimmer, Deanna Hill, and Shana Pribesh, *Inspiration, Perspiration, and Time: Operations and Achievement in Edison Schools*, Santa Monica, Calif.: RAND Corporation, MG-351-EDU, 2005. As of November 5, 2008:
http://www.rand.org/pubs/monographs/MG351/

Gill, Brian, P. Mike Timpane, Karen E. Ross, Dominic J. Brewer, and Kevin Booker, *Rhetoric Versus Reality: What We Know and What We Need to Know About Vouchers and Charter Schools*, Santa Monica, Calif.: RAND Corporation, MR-1118-1-EDU, 2007. As of November 5, 2008:
http://www.rand.org/pubs/monograph_reports/MR1118-1/

Grogger, Jeffrey, and Derek Neal, "Further Evidence on the Effects of Catholic Secondary Schooling," *Brookings-Wharton Papers on Urban Affairs, 2000*, Washington, D.C.: Brookings Institution Press, 2000, pp. 151–201.

Gronberg, Timothy J., and Dennis W. Jansen, *Navigating Newly Chartered Waters: An Analysis of Texas Charter School Performance*, San Antonio, Tex.: Texas Public Policy Foundation, April 2001.

Hamilton, Laura, "Assessment as a Policy Tool," *Review of Research in Education*, Vol. 27, 2003, pp. 25–68.

Hanushek, Eric Alan, John F. Kain, Steven G. Rivkin, and Gregory F. Branch, *Charter School Quality and Parental Decision Making with School Choice*, Cambridge, Mass.: National Bureau of Economic Research working paper 11252, March 2005. As of February 4, 2009:
http://www.nber.org/papers/W11252

Hess, Frederick M., *Spinning Wheels: The Politics of Urban School Reform*, Washington, D.C.: Brookings Institution Press, 1999.

Hess, G. Alfred, *Restructuring Urban Schools: A Chicago Perspective*, New York: Teachers College Press, Teachers College, Columbia University, 1995.

Hill, Carolyn J., Howard S. Bloom, Alison Rebeck Black, and Mark W. Lipsey, *Empirical Benchmarks for Interpreting Effect Sizes in Research*, New York: MDRC, July 2007. As of November 5, 2008:
http://www.mdrc.org/publications/459/abstract.html

Hill, Paul T., Gail E. Foster, and Tamar Gendler, *High Schools with Character*, Santa Monica, Calif.: RAND Corporation, R-3944-RC, August 1990. As of February 4, 2009:
http://www.rand.org/pubs/reports/R3944/

Hill, Paul Thomas, Lawrence C. Pierce, and James W. Guthrie, *Reinventing Public Education: How Contracting Can Transform America's Schools*, Chicago, Ill.: University of Chicago Press, 1997.

Holmes, George Mark, Jeff DeSimone, and Nicholas G. Rupp, *Does School Choice Increase School Quality?* Cambridge, Mass.: National Bureau of Economic Research working paper 9683, May 2003. As of November 5, 2008:
http://www.nber.org/papers/w9683

Hoxby, Caroline Minter, *School Choice and School Productivity (or Could School Choice Be a Tide That Lifts All Boats?)*, Cambridge, Mass.: National Bureau of Economic Research, working paper 8873, 2002. As of February 10, 2009:
http://www.nber.org/papers/w8873

———, *A Straightforward Comparison of Charter Schools and Regular Public Schools in the United States*, Cambridge, Mass.: National Bureau of Economic Research, September 2004.

Hoxby, Caroline Minter, and Sonali Murarka, *Methods of Assessing the Achievement of Students in Charter Schools*, delivered at the National Conference on Charter School Research, Vanderbilt University, Nashville, Tenn., September 28, 2006. As of November 5, 2008:
http://www.vanderbilt.edu/schoolchoice/conference/papers/Hoxby-Murarka_2006-DRAFT.pdf

———, *Charter Schools in New York City: Who Enrolls and How They Affect Their Students' Achievement*, Cambridge, Mass: National Bureau of Economic Research, June 2007. As of November 5, 2008:
http://www.nber.org/~schools/charterschoolseval/nyc_charter_schools_technical_report_july2007.pdf

Hoxby, Caroline Minter, and Jonah E. Rockoff, *The Impact of Charter Schools on Student Achievement*, Cambridge, Mass.: Harvard University Department of Economics, and New York: Columbia University Business School, November 2004.

Imberman, Scott A., *Achievement and Behavior in Charter Schools: Drawing a More Complete Picture*, Houston, Tex.: University of Houston, September 28, 2007. As of February 5, 2009:
http://www.ncspe.org/publications_files/OP142.pdf

Krueger, Alan B., "Experimental Estimates of Education Production Functions," *Quarterly Journal of Economics*, Vol. 114, No. 2, May 1999, pp. 497–532.

Levene, H., "Robust Tests for Equality of Variances," in Ingram Olkin, Sudhist G. Ghurye, Wassily Hoeffding, William G. Madow, and Henry B. Mann, eds., *Contributions to Probability and Statistics: Essays in Honor of Harold Hotelling*, Stanford, Calif.: Stanford University Press, 1960, pp. 278–292.

Maddala, G. S., *Limited-Dependent and Qualitative Variables in Econometrics*, Cambridge, UK: Cambridge University Press, 1983.

Mathematica Policy Research, "Charter Schools: Are They Effective?" undated Web page. As of February 4, 2009:
http://www.mathematica-mpr.com/education/charterschools.asp

Mathews, Jay, *Work Hard. Be Nice: How Two Inspired Teachers Created the Most Promising Schools in America*, Chapel Hill, N.C.: Algonquin Books, 2009.

May, Henry, Jonathan A. Supovitz, and David Perda, *A Longitudinal Study of the Impact of America's Choice on Student Performance in Rochester, New York, 1998–2003*, Philadelphia, Pa.: Consortium for Policy Research in Education, University of Pennsylvania, Graduate School of Education, July 2004. As of February 5, 2009:
http://www.cpre.org/images/stories/cpre_pdfs/AC-10.pdf

McClure, Larry, Betsy Strick, Rachel Jacob-Almeida, and Christopher Reicher, *The Preuss School at UCSD: School Characteristics and Students' Achievement*, San Diego, Calif.: Center for Research on Educational Equity, Assessment and Teaching Excellence, University of California, September 2005. As of February 10, 2009:
http://create.ucsd.edu/Research_Evaluation/PreussReportDecember2005.pdf

Mead, Sara, and Andrew J. Rotherham, *A Sum Greater Than the Parts: What States Can Teach Each Other About Charter Schooling*, Washington, D.C.: Education Sector, September 2007. As of February 5, 2009:
http://www.educationsector.org/research/research_show.htm?doc_id=521913

Miron, Gary, and Christopher D. Nelson, *What's Public About Charter Schools? Lessons Learned About Choice and Accountability*, Thousand Oaks, Calif.: Corwin Press, 2002.

National Student Clearinghouse, undated home page. As of February 5, 2009:
http://www.studentclearinghouse.org/

Neal, Derek, "The Effects of Catholic Secondary Schooling on Educational Achievement," *Journal of Labor Economics*, Vol. 15, No. 1, January 1997, pp. 98–123.

Nelson, F. Howard, Bella Rosenberg, and Nancy Van Meter, *Charter School Achievement on the 2003 National Assessment of Educational Progress*, Washington, D.C.: American Federation of Teachers, August 2004. As of February 4, 2009:
http://www.aft.org/pubs-reports/downloads/teachers/NAEPCharterSchoolReport.pdf

Ohio Department of Education, "Community School Legislative History," *2006–2007 Annual Report on Ohio Community Schools*, December 31, 2007, pp. 16–26. As of February 13, 2009:
http://www.ode.state.oh.us/GD/DocumentManagement/DocumentDownload.aspx?DocumentID=41920

Powell, Judith, Jose Blackorby, Julie Marsh, Kara Finnegan, and Lee Anderson, *Evaluation of Charter School Effectiveness*, Menlo Park, Calif.: SRI International, December 11, 1997. As of February 4, 2009:
http://bibpurl.oclc.org/web/9140

Ross, Steven, J. Nunnery, and L. J. Smith, *Evaluation of Elementary School-Wide Programs: Clover Park School District Year 1: 1996–97*, Memphis, Tenn.: University of Memphis, Center for Research in Educational Policy, 1996.

Ross, Steven, William Sanders, S. Paul Wright, Sam Stringfield, L. Weiping Wang, and Marty Alberg, "Two- and Three-Year Achievement Results from the Memphis Restructuring Initiative," *School Effectiveness and School Improvement*, Vol. 12, No. 3, 2001, pp. 323–346.

Russo, Alexander W. W., *A Tough Nut to Crack in Ohio: Charter Schooling in the Buckeye State*, Washington, D.C.: Progressive Policy Institute, PPI policy report, February 1, 2005. As of February 10, 2009:
http://www.ppionline.org/ppi_ci.cfm?knlgAreaID=110&subsecID=134&contentID=253140

Sander, William, and Anthony C. Krautmann, "Catholic Schools, Dropout Rates and Educational Attainment," *Economic Inquiry*, Vol. 33, No. 2, April 1995, pp. 217–233.

Sass, Tim R., "Charter Schools and Student Achievement in Florida," *Education Finance and Policy*, Vol. 1, No. 1, Winter 2006, pp. 91–122. As of February 4, 2009:
http://www.mitpressjournals.org/doi/pdf/10.1162/edfp.2006.1.1.91

Shober, Arnold F., Paul Manna, and John F. Witte, "Flexibility Meets Accountability: State Charter School Laws and Their Influence on the Formation of Charter Schools in the United States," *Policy Studies Journal*, Vol. 34, No. 4, November 2006, pp. 563–587.

Sizer, Theodore R., *Horace's School: Redesigning the American High School*, Boston, Mass.: Houghton Mifflin Co., 1992.

Slavin, Robert E., Nancy A. Madden, Nancy L. Karweit, Lawrence J. Dolan, and Barbara A. Wasik, "Success for All: A Comprehensive Approach to Prevention and Early Intervention," in Robert E. Slavin, Nancy L. Karweit, and Barbara A. Wasik, eds., *Preventing Early School Failure: Research, Policy, and Practice*, Boston, Mass.: Allyn and Bacon, 1994.

Solmon, Lewis C., Kern Paark, and David Garcia, "Does Charter School Attendance Improve Test Scores? The Arizona Results," *Arizona Education Analysis*, March 16, 2001. As of February 4, 2009:
http://www.goldwaterinstitute.org/AboutUs/ArticleView.aspx?id=111

Summers, Anita A., and Barbara L. Wolfe, "Do Schools Make a Difference?" *American Economic Review*, Vol. 67, No. 4, September 1977, pp. 639–652.

Thomas B. Fordham Institute, *Charter School Funding: Inequity's Next Frontier*, Washington, D.C.: Thomas B. Fordham Institute, Progress Analytics Institute, and Public Impact, 2005. As of February 10, 2009:
http://www.edexcellence.net/doc/Charter%20School%20Funding%202005%20FINAL.pdf

Toma, Eugenia F., Ron Zimmer, and J. Jones, "Beyond Achievement: Enrollment Consequences of Charter Schools in Michigan," in Timothy Gronberg and Dennis W. Jansen, eds., *Advances in Applied Microeconomics*, Vol. 14: *Improving School Accountability: Check-Ups or Choice*, Amsterdam: Elsevier Science, 2006.

UCLA Charter School Study, *Beyond the Rhetoric of Charter School Reform: A Study of Ten California School Districts*, Los Angeles, Calif., 1999.

Whitman, David, *Sweating the Small Stuff: Inner-City Schools and the New Paternalism*, Washington, D.C.: Thomas B. Fordham Institute, 2008. As of February 10, 2009:
http://www.edexcellence.net/doc/20080826-sweating-the-small-stuff.pdf

Witte, John, David Weimer, Arnold Shober, and Paul Schlomer, "The Performance of Charter Schools in Wisconsin," *Journal of Policy Analysis and Management*, Vol. 26, No. 3, Summer 2007, pp. 557–573.

Zimmer, Ron, Suzanne Blanc, Brian Gill, and Jolley Christman, *Evaluating the Performance of Philadelphia's Charter Schools*, Santa Monica, Calif.: RAND Corporation, WR-550-WPF, 2008. As of February 13, 2009:
http://www.rand.org/pubs/working_papers/WR550/

Zimmer, Ron W., and Richard Buddin, "Charter School Performance in Two Large Urban Districts," *Journal of Urban Economics*, Vol. 60, No. 2, 2006, pp. 307–326.

———, "Getting Inside the Black Box: Examining How the Operation of Charter Schools Affects Performance," *Peabody Journal of Education*, Vol. 82, Nos. 2–3, 2007, pp. 231–273.

Zimmer, Ron, Richard Buddin, Derrick Chau, Glenn A. Daley, Brian Gill, Cassandra M. Guarino, Laura S. Hamilton, Cathy Krop, Daniel F. McCaffrey, Melinda Sandler, and Dominic J. Brewer, *Charter School Operations and Performance: Evidence from California*, Santa Monica, Calif.: RAND Corporation, MR-1700-EDU, 2003. As of November 5, 2008:
http://www.rand.org/pubs/monograph_reports/MR1700/

Zimmer, Ron W., and Eugenia F. Toma, "Peer Effects in Private and Public Schools Across Countries," *Journal of Policy Analysis and Management*, Vol. 19, No. 1, Winter 2000, pp. 75–92.